INTO THE SECRET HEART OF ASHDOWN FOREST: A HORSEMAN'S COUNTRY DIARY

INTO THE SECRET HEART OF ASHDOWN FOREST: A HORSEMAN'S COUNTRY DIARY

JULIAN ROUP

ILLUSTRATED BY ABBIE HART

www.blkdogpublishing.com

Also by Julian Roup:

Life in a Time of Plague:
A Coronavirus Lockdown Diary

Life in a Time of Plague is the story of Britain under the first 75 days of its unprecedented Covid-19 lockdown, seen from the author's rural East Sussex valley home in England.

From the refuge of a seemingly idyllic rural idyll, the book monitors in bleak and forensic detail the failure of the Government to protect Britain, and its woeful response at every stage of the pandemic.

The author's age and medical issues colour this diary with a dark humour, as his age group is most at risk. He is determined to make his 70th birthday at least, despite the thousands of deaths in Britain to date.

It is a quiet slow appreciation of the bright green spring and summer of 2020 in the English countryside, set against the horrors faced by frontline workers. However, what is most surprising is that amid the death, heartache and economic carnage, there is also a silver lining, a chance to simply stop and stare, and rethink our lives.

Praise for *Life in a Time of Plague*

"It is a wonderful account of the time of coronavirus; I especially like the reverie at the end with its sense of time regained in that Proustian way. Julian Roup has a great gift for evocation and description."
Bernard O'Donoghue, Whitbread Prize winning Irish poet, Oxford don, author of *Seamus Heaney and the Language of Poetry*.

"Witty, incisive, irreverent, iconoclastic."
George Plumptre, CEO National Garden Scheme, author of *The English Country House Garden* and *Royal Gardens of Europe*.

"Journalist Julian Roup tells the story of his corner of rural Britain under the first 75 days of lockdown. His beautiful writing captures the way the world slowed down amid the strangeness of the new reality. The book is a snapshot of the details that make up the fabric of history – thinking back on memories of friends passed, observations on humanity and the natural world in his East Sussex valley, and of course his lovely horse Callum. Riders will appreciate how horses – in both reality and in our imagination – serve as an escape."
Horse & Hound.

Praise for *Fisherman in the Saddle*

"This is story telling charged with raw emotion and always a deep appreciation for the sheer beauty and the enduring magic of nature which transcends politics, implosion of families, emigration. Horses, the author says, became 'my nation, my friends, my identity, my medicine. When I am in the saddle I'm home."
Robyn Cohen, *The Cape Times*.

"Every now and then a gem of a new book lands on my desk: sometimes but rarely a diamond. This is one. I laughed. I

cried. I was deeply moved. This is among the best books I have ever read about fishing, horses, growing up, the pain of maturity, leaving one's homeland and the things that make up the richness of life."
Dave Bristow, *Getaway Magazine*.

"The ability of horses to help and heal is boundless. In A Fisherman in the Saddle, Julian Roup explains how he feels about horses. 'The feeling of elation, of freedom, of excitement was indescribable. It was like being given wings and the gift of flight. I was hooked for life.' I know the feeling, and I hope many others discover it for themselves."
Octavia Pollock, *Country Life*.

Praise for *Boerejood*

"Brilliant, just terrific, really very, very good. Engaged, intelligent, personal, fast moving and funny."
Graham Watts, *Financial Times*, London.

"A delicate exploration of a society 10 years after the end of apartheid and the onset of majority rule. Roup has no nostalgia for the old regime, but immense sadness for the embattlement of the Afrikaans language and culture."
John Lloyd, Editor, *FT Weekend Magazine*.

For Jan, Dom and Steph:

My safety net in the plague years of 2020 -2021.

Julian and Callum
© Janice Warman

Abbie and Alfred

Acknowledgements

I wish to thank my first readers and cheer group Jay and Guy Louw. I also wish to thank Julia Nye, a horse riding friend and neighbour, for suggesting Abbie Hart as an illustrator. My thanks to Abbie for her wonderful images which so enrich the book. Thanks to my wife Jan for endless advice, encouragement and superb editing. And thanks to Zoe Sibson for good company out riding and for taking care of Callum when I was shielding from Covid-19.

WAKING UP,
SLOWING DOWN

Julian Roup

I wake at 6am as usual, but today there is silence here in the High Weald on Ashdown Forest. There is no dawn chorus. The weeks of impassioned birdsong that gladdened the start of my early spring and summer days are over. The birds have established territories, found a mate and are nesting. The wedding season is over, the honeymoon history.

The years of commuting to London each working day lives on in my mind, setting a subconscious alarm clock ringing at 6am sharp, each morning. These last five years since leaving Bonhams, the international fine art auction house, have meant I can have a lie-in, there is no rush to the shower, the car, the train waiting at Tunbridge Wells station nine miles north and then the hour's train ride to London, sitting among workers packed like beans in a tin. There is no frantic listening to the news in the car, scanning the newspapers on the train for a mention of Bonhams or its competitors, which is how my day as Director of Press and Marketing started each day. The awkward page-turning of newspapers in the train carriage, with my elbows held close to my side, embarrassment and anxiety my closest companions, just below my clothes. This before online news relieved me of that burden.

Now I lie in bed after making coffee and listen, just listen. Birdsong returns slowly but it is there, faintly at first and then more robustly, but it has a conversational tone now, rather than the urgent opera of the past weeks. Even after 40 years in this English country place, I do not know what I am listening to; I do not know the names of my avian neighbours unless I see them and, even then, I am not sure if I know their names. The handful of birds I can identify include robins, magpies, crows, blackbirds, wood pigeons, kestrels, buzzards, swallows, blue tits and woodpeckers. The wrens, wagtails and the rest, I am less sure of. And there are others that I hear but do not see, like the cuckoo and the skylark. My sightings, such as they are, remain glimpses, ghostly flashes. But I know they are there. And at dusk there are other aerial shapes above me, the bats and the owls, weaving their way through the corridors of dusk and then deeper into the night.

It is a privilege, hard won, to lie here in bed and simply listen, coffee in hand. The air about the cottage is no longer just the preserve of birds; now it is crowded with flies, butterflies, midges, ladybirds and all manner of flying insects that I don't have names for either. I am a very imperfect naturalist. The flying insects don't bother me much; they are there, but few and far between to my human eyes. Not the pest they are in Scotland and other northern places, where the short summers mean an explosion of insect life and a trial for humans unused to it.

Hunger gets me out of bed a second time to go down to the kitchen to make breakfast, marmalade, toast and coffee as usual. Later, I walk down the hill to see my horse Callum and as I stroll in the already warm day, I become aware of the swallows winnowing the paddocks for insects, swooping low among the horses and then rocketing up again, their motion a roller coaster ride on wings, a trajectory of their choosing. What a way to live in this world, describing arabesques in the air, feather light. No horizon finite, everything yours, every destination a possibility, no airports, no packing, no passports, no squashing in alongside other suffering souls. Just the vast open skies and the sun.

My sister Jay and her husband Guy, who live in Cape Town, South Africa, had a son named Kirsten, an ornithologist-naturalist by trade, who took himself off at the age of 26 and never came back. But he left his affairs in impeccable order and among his effects were all the paraphernalia and accoutrements of the professional birder he was, who had criss-crossed sub-Saharan Africa learning his fieldcraft. I spoke at his funeral, although like Macavity he was not there, just an aching hole in the hearts of those who loved him. The why of it remains a why to this day, 15 years gone. A flower he discovered bears his name.

As I write now, I can clearly feel his slightly waspish presence as he looks over my shoulder. I tell him he chose to go, so he has no right to torment those of us who are still labouring in this vineyard. He pays me no heed whatsoever. Just groans from the pit of his stomach. In some strange way that his parents, his close friends and I cannot fathom, he has not truly left. He haunts us with his presence. Apparently, St Augustine said, 'The dead are invisible, not absent.' So true.

Jay used to ask Kirsten, 'How do I get good at birding? QUICKLY!!' And he told her, 'You have to keep looking. Just keep looking.' She says, 'I'm by no means a good birder, but I look, every day, and I see things that gladden my heart, or sadden it, as the case may be.' So her advice to me is, 'Keep looking! And look things up and see how every bit of nature is dependent on another bit, and how it leads you from species to species, to conservation, to the well-being of the planet. And then of course, there is our species. Watch them too, they are endlessly fascinating!' I intend to try, despite Kirsten's 'noises off', as the playwright Alan Ayckbourn might have put it.

So in these pieces about Ashdown Forest in Sussex, I am going to try to fill the aching cavity, the Kirsten-shaped void, one he should have filled with books himself, of great and particular erudition, and his own brand of acerbic humour. Some of it at my expense. But however ham-handed, I am going to have a shot at becoming a very imperfect observer on my rides through Ashdown Forest.

Julian Roup

Into the Secret Heart of Ashdown Forest

Julian Roup

There are days in which my horse riding on Ashdown Forest takes me to the wide-open heathlands that make up the majority of the 6,500 acres of this green paradise. These open, rolling miles are the busy, popular part of the Forest, well served with car parks, giving dog walkers easy access to its paths, benches with views and ice-cream vans, its heights crowned by the Forest's iconic emblem, its dark pine circles. My riding here is a fairly social event, with many greetings and the odd chat with walkers.

I am aware that my big chestnut gelding Callum and my presence in this part of the Forest presents both pleasure and annoyance to the walkers. They often need to catch their dogs to put them on leads to prevent them barking at or harrying the horse, and this breaks up the peaceful nature of their walk. Some do it graciously, commenting, 'Safe rather than sorry!' as I ride by and I thank them kindly for their trouble. Others are plainly irritated, taciturn and don't even look at me when I thank them for collaring their hounds.

Other walkers, who are riders themselves, or simply love horses, will often comment on Callum's beauty. 'He's a magnificent horse! How many hands?' and I am more than delighted to accept the compliment on his behalf, which often leads to discussions about his breeding and the walker's own experience of horses and riding.

This is enriching for all concerned and Callum welcomes the chance to simply stand and stare, looking noble, while he catches his breath. These days he is so used to this occurrence that he starts to slow down when he sees walkers approaching, knowing they could well give him a chance to halt and chill. On a warm summer's day, this kind of ride has its pleasures without doubt.

But then there are times in which I choose to immerse myself in the primordial woods, the last remaining vestiges of the Forest of Anderida that made southern Britain well-nigh impenetrable for centuries before the arrival of the Romans led by Julius Caesar in 55 BC and their subsequent raids and final conquest of England beginning in AD 41. This led to a road being punched through the Forest from London to the south coast. These rides into the Forest's secret depths are an altogether different experience. It is about silence, secrecy, wildness, and worship.

Six months on from my ruminations in bed, coffee in hand, listening to muted summer birdsong, the season has turned. Yesterday was 2 December 2020, a bright, cold, sunny day on which it was announced that a vaccine for Covid-19, the pandemic that had brought the world to an almost year-long halt, was being rolled out with immediate effect. It was the news the whole country had been waiting for with various degrees of patience and panic, fear of death and loathing of the lockdown which so inhibited our freedoms.

I chose to ride into the heavily wooded part of the Forest for a bit of 'forest bathing' as the Japanese like to call forest worship, so good for the soul. Callum and I dropped down the back hill behind our cottage, over the river bridge and turned right, following the stream to a point just above a river crossing 'splash' and then steeply uphill to the Church Hill car park on the road that goes to Mardens Hill and on to Friar's Gate and Lye Green. And once we were across this country road, we ducked through the huge holly hedge into the woods proper, owned by the De La Warr family who have signs everywhere saying, 'Private Keep Out'.

As I have been riding this patch for 37 years, I feel I have earned a commoner's right of way even though recently I have been stopped twice by the land agent who works for the De La Warrs, and reminded (politely, it must be said), that this is private land. My response, equally polite, was to explain that I have been riding here for almost four decades with no previous problem at all and I was under the impression that the Wealden Way which crosses this area gave me a right of access.

This did not wash, and he said so. The second time I saw him, some weeks later, we had an altogether more amicable discussion when I revealed my age and heart condition and that I felt these rides of my mine were a sort of farewell to the Forest. This elicited the admission that he was in recovery from health issues and well understood my feeling and that I should continue with my ride, which I did, after thanking him and wishing him well.

So, taking heart from this very human exchange in the woods, Callum and I set our course for the very heart of Five Hundred Acre Wood.

As you move through the wood on Forest tracks, you pass deer hides in certain trees, accessed by ladders which allow shooters a good view over glades and clearings, offering a clear shot of the deer endemic to this area. A certain amount of culling goes on and although I have never seen a gunman, I have heard the occasional shot.

We passed the clearing where felled logs have been stacked for some months now, curing and awaiting collection. Then down a long Forest ride flanked by pines and deciduous Forest and brown drying banks of bracken, and so towards the crossing into the publicly owned land bought by the East Sussex Council after the hurricane of 1987 that caused so much destruction. This so depressed the De La Warrs that they sold up the major part of Ashdown Forest to the local authority. Every cloud has a silver lining, as they say.

The Earl De La Warr holds the subsidiary titles of Viscount Cantelupe (1761) in the Peerage of Great Britain; Baron De La Warr (1572) in the Peerage of England; and Baron Buckhurst, of Buckhurst in the County of Sussex (1864) in the Peerage of the United Kingdom.

In Britain, the public have a right of access to just eight per cent of the countryside. This green and pleasant land remains in the control of a handful of owners, many of whom received their land gift from William the Conqueror and subsequent kings. Britain may be a democracy, but the countryside has never shaken off its feudal past. It is another world.

This does not overly concern the Forest denizens we pass – the rabbits, deer, squirrels and the pairs of buzzards criss-crossing the Forest skies. They give us a glance and carry on with their lives.

At this point I had a decision to make: to take the usual path uphill or, for the first time in years, head downhill in an attempt to reach the road to Hartfield where I would connect with a good bridleway back onto the open Forest. This decision to go down the hill presented a serious challenge as this part of the Forest has not been cleared since the hurricane of 1987 and many fallen trees block the now overgrown path down through dense wood. I decided to give it a shot as Callum has proven himself steady and sure-footed when 'bundu bashing', as they say in South Africa, my birthplace.

Now began a careful slow descent, pushing aside branches, stepping over fallen trees, circling round larger fallen giants by moving into the bracken while keeping a sharp lookout for crevices, boggy bits or snags underfoot. Callum was calm and careful. We made good progress and by and by we came to an earthen rampart that blocked our progress downhill but allowed us to slant left, south into the Forest still moving downhill but at a tangent.

Now and then we stopped to give ourselves a breather from the work of branch breaking and endless detours. Callum stood rocklike listening to the sounds of the Forest, the sighing of the wind high above us in the treetops, and the rustle of foraging squirrels and small birds about us. Then lifting the reins once more, I headed onward. It was clear that no one had been this way for decades, the moss on the fallen trees was pristine, and the only marks on the land were the thin trails left by deer.

We then came to a place where there was a mini-ravine that we had to cross, or be forced to go back. I cast around for the easiest crossing point where the earthen cut was at its narrowest, and the horse jumped across it easily. Now we found ourselves in a more open, cathedral-like Forest with much less undergrowth impeding our progress. Here and there stood enormous holly trees with nothing growing beneath them, and truly giant beeches and oaks. We threaded our way through them, the lie of the land forcing us now back uphill helped by well-trodden deer-paths.

And then something inexplicable happened. A presence quite unseen, but felt, was in the clearing with us. I felt a shiver down my spine and the hairs on my arms stood erect. Callum felt it too. He changed instantly from being totally relaxed to high alert, his head up, airs pricked, nostrils wide, smelling the air, haunches bunched, ready for flight. I held him steady as a mad gallop through the wood would doubtless not have ended well for us. We moved uphill swiftly now, super-alert to every sound and sight. The presence we both felt was not threatening, it was just there. We had gone from being the only ones on the Forest to sharing it with something we could not see. I can only say that it felt as though the Forest acknowledged us; it was a spirit of place, rather than anything human or dark. As we moved higher, the feeling subsided, and we were alone again.

About 45 minutes from the decision to turn downhill at the gate, we emerged at the top of the Forest into a clearing I knew well, home to a 'family' of great beech trees with one bearing a massive fungal growth, my place of prayer and meditation. We stopped and breathed in this known space and the horse relaxed, put his head down and nibbled at leaves and grass. I looked back at the way we had come but it was blocked off by holly bushes; the reality we had passed through had not followed us but had remained in its own realm, the very heart of the Forest.

I collected Callum and we started a long, slow canter up a grassy track that took us out of the wood into open moorland, releasing the tension in both of us. But the sense of other stayed with me all day and as I got into bed that night, lying in the dark thinking about the ride, I felt a thrill at what I had been privileged to experience in the heart of the Forest. No doubt we will go back. It is not often that a forest speaks to you.

Julian Roup

Ashdown Forest Magic

Julian Roup

After 40 years of walking and riding Ashdown Forest, it is hardly surprising that I think the place is magic and a place of magic too. How else to explain the life force one finds out in the woods? How to share the sense of reinvigoration when crossing its miles on a walk or a ride?

Truly, to quote the song: The Teddy Bears Picnic:

'If you go down in the woods today
You're sure of a big surprise,
If you go down in the woods today,
You'd better go in disguise!'

There is a truth in those words I would not have imagined until I washed up in these parts back in 1980. Over the years, I've heard talk of magic hereabouts; ley lines on the Forest, white magic, witchcraft and the fact that this area seems to be a haven for alternative lifestyles and religions. Within a ten-mile radius of our home, there are communities of Rosicrucians, Mormons, Catholic Monasteries and retreats, Scientologists, Opus Dei and Druids.

I don't pay much heed to any of this, but it is very hard to spend some hours out in the deepest reaches of Ashdown Forest and not connect with something primordial as well as spiritual. It may just be the fact that here nature is still paramount, which is surprising, given that the Forest is smack bang in the middle of such a crowded place. But, like a whirlpool, it pulls you into its own reality and it's easy to feel something different here. There is magic, both light and dark.

It's not the teddy bears picnicking that you will find is the surprise, but the trees, the rare heathland, the gorse and the silver birches, the variety of mushrooms and the streams and their crossings. The Forest has much to teach us and to surprise us with.

I've come across some very strange things over the

years while out riding. You cover a lot of ground on a horse in two or three hours – eight to twelve miles roll by easily. And now and again something has stopped me dead in my tracks. A crucified crow; a child's plastic doll with bird's feathers poking out of the eye sockets; strange constructions of wooden lean-tos with circles before them; and once near Pooh Sticks Bridge, a fully-dressed male mannequin, seemingly a suicide, hanging in a tree. Maybe someone having strange fun, wishing to give passers-by the willies, or maybe something darker. I will never know.

The Forest, of course, is home to the redcap Fly Agaric mushroom, often associated with witches. Deadly nightshade or *Atropa Belladonna*, and foxgloves, whose botanical name is *Digitalis purpurea*, a poison loved by the crime-writer Agatha Christie, grow here too. It is a landscape of toxic plants and mind-altering mushrooms, amid the innocent vegetation.

Herds of deer move through these woods. If you are on a horse, they will move off the path some yards and once in cover, they will stop and turn to observe your passing. Many eyes in the gloom.

There is an abiding silence in some areas. And in others the Forest is clothed in green moss. There are areas that are well-nigh impenetrable and then there are the majestic cathedral-like spaces amid giant beeches. Foxes and adders and badgers live here too. And pairs of buzzards quarter the fields and woods, looking for both the quick and the dead.

The magic I speak of and find in the Forest is not from man but from nature. When you ride among trees as I do, you ride among beings older, far older than you. And though they don't move from their position, they feel and observe movement constantly, the movement of wind, of rain, of the sun, the moon and the stars and human and animal passersby. They are rooted deep in the soil, yet they are beings of the air and the sky, and their music is that of the wind through their branches. To be among trees is to be aware of the slowing of your frenetic human mind to something calmer, more akin to a tree's state of quiet consciousness. That is magic enough.

And then there is the magic of light through the leaves and branches of a wood. The Forest cloud cover is ever changing and brings with it a movement of light that gilds the hills and valleys. Sunsets and sunrises provide their own drama and interest.

Because we don't suffer the light pollution you get in a city, the nights are themselves an opportunity to observe the display of starlight and moonlight across the Forest. About a week ago, just before heading for bed, I felt the need of some fresh air and went and stood in the garden for some minutes. I was met by the most fantastic light show provided by fast moving, low, broken cloud, racing below a full moon. This ever-changing vista, seen from the darkness beneath the pines and beeches that fringe our garden, was spectacular and the feeling it engendered was not dissimilar to the effect of the operatic aria, *Nessun Dorma*, (Let no one sleep), from the final act of Puccini's opera *Turandot*. I felt half whirled into an ecstasy beneath this light show. I felt my heart, spirit and soul lift as it never does in any place of worship other than the Forest. If this is not powerful magic, then I don't know what is.

I have crossed the Forest's rolling miles across four decades in states of grief, of sadness, of heartbreak and of fear, and I've come to it too in states of joy of gladness of happiness and contentment. Always, always, without fail, it holds itself out to you with comfort and companionship. Our human love for the Forest is returned in more than equal measure.

We are never entirely alone on the Forest. The dead lie thick about us here. In every beauty spot, human ashes are scattered. I have been at two funeral sites where the ashes of a very old woman and a young woman lie scattered.

There is the Airman's Grave too, with the fatal hill behind it, and to the south, the open skies to the South Downs and beyond them the Channel and France. The grave holds no bodies but commemorates the deaths of six young RAF airmen in the Second World War whose aircraft, a Wellington Mk II W5364 QT-H, returning from a bombing raid on Cologne, ended its homeward journey here in fire and destruction on the last day of July 1941, impacting the Forest at this site. Passing by, I always stop to say thank you for their sacrifice.

For me, the very heart of the Forest's magic is its power to restore the spirit, never more so than now, in my eighth decade, following heart surgery, and in the disease-blighted year of 2020. A potential death sentence provided me with a new lease of life. Facing the inevitable made me think hard about priorities and one of the first things I did post-recovery from surgery was to buy a new horse, Callum. Looking after him, feeding, grooming, mucking out and riding, has kept me fit and given me the chance to renew and deepen my love affair with the Forest, criss-crossing its every mile like an old wolf marking his territory. If this be magic, so be it.

Sadly, I know, it must end one day, this stitching of my life to the Forest, and I would not be human if that thought does not grieve me. But I would not have it any other way. Horses and the Forest this last 40 years have been central to my life and my wellbeing. Saying farewell will be hard.

NO SUCH THING AS BAD WEATHER

Julian Roup

W hen we first arrived here from the heat and light of a South African Cape summer in 1980, to say that I found the weather a challenge would be to understate the true state of things. I grieved for home and I missed its weather. This state lasted many years.

Then one day I heard the expression from Alfred Wainwright, the great walker and writer of the outdoors in the Lake District. 'There is no such thing as bad weather, only unsuitable clothing.' and I thought he had a point, but I also thought it was a big fat lie. I hated going outdoors in any kind of inclement weather.

But after some months in Sussex, we bought horses as a way to help us settle in and it worked like magic. We geared up with the right clothing; it was that or pneumonia and death. Waterproofs, suede chaps, wax jackets, gloves. My mother sent me long johns too. And we soon enough realised that once you were properly clothed and on horseback, the weather was really much less of an issue. In fact, being out in the wind and rain could be exhilarating, and you had the place to yourself.

The days of looking out the window, shuddering and going back to bed or getting another coffee and returning to the couch were over! There were horses to feed, muck out, groom and exercise, wind, rain or shine, before, after and during work. Our immersion into England started in earnest.

After three years of riding on the South Downs, where there is no place to hide from the wind and rain, we discovered Ashdown Forest and took a giant step for this family, finally beginning to put roots down. The forest was a revelation with its wide-open reaches, big skies, commanding views from its almost 1,000-foot height and just as much its hidden secret places, its woods and dells, its streams, its valley floors, the many places a walker or rider could hide from the storm.

After some more years of riding here, I made a surprising discovery. I got less wet here than in the Cape. People think of the Cape in terms of its glorious Mediterranean-style summers but forget its ice cold, biting wet winters below that grey, brooding granite giant, table mountain, which sucks in moisture off the south Atlantic and dumps it in cloudbursts that feel as though they could flatten a car roof. I have been caught out in too many of them to mention. The horse I was riding, almost frantic with the violence, ears laid back, head shaking, and streaming water as stair-rods hammered down, and then bounced six foot back off the ground so that it hit you twice – once on the way down and once more on the way back up. It was hellish.

In comparison, English rain is mostly mizzle. Admittedly, it can last for days, sometimes it seems for weeks and months, but it does not have the malicious fury of the Cape of Storms.

So with judicious shopping at the South of England Show and Hickstead and the local tack shops, we geared up for the Sussex weather. What you wear tells a lot about you. I'm one of those who lives in jeans and a fleece. Clothes are not a big part of my concerns.

I remember some years ago walking past the DIY stable yard next door on my way to dinner with near neighbours. A friend, bringing a gelding in for the night, said with a grin, 'Gosh, you brush up well!' I was not sure whether to be flattered or insulted. Do I look such a scruff usually, I wondered? Probably, yes.

The point is that I'm more concerned about what I wear when out riding. It's a tricky business getting it right. After all, this is a climate that can and does produce four seasons on any given day of the year. So if you are out riding for any length of time, you want to be sure you are well prepared. The weather forecast can be useful at times, and then there are occasions when it's more of a handicap. It sets you up for sunshine and rewards you with a hailstorm.

The careful, comfort-loving horseman must give up some time to contemplating this issue. Headgear is easy – a riding helmet. Not ideal in the wet – an Australian bush-hat would do much better in keeping off the rain – but they tend to blow off, while a helmet has life-saving qualities. So it's a hard hat. Until quite recently, mine was black velvet covered, going brown with age, and not that useful in a fall. I have now invested in one of the new British Horse Society approved crash helmets, which is extremely comfortable and offers better protection.

I have a good selection of warm winter shirts, a dozen jerseys in various states, weights and quality. Jeans are easy, as they save one from having to change into breeches or jodhpurs. Then there are boots – Muckers for winter and leather ankle boots for summer, both carrying blunt dressage spurs, there to keep the engine at the horse's back-end connected to the legs in front, a considerable task with Callum, who is quite happy to slop along on the forehand, the back trailing free. Not a good idea in the wet, or on the Forest's rutted paths.

Then there are the two key additions that experience makes me favour – leather chaps and a waxed jacket. A transatlantic fusion, you might say. The leather chaps keep your jeans clean and your legs warm and dry. And then the waxed jacket, that most useful of English inventions, which is warm, waterproof and which breathes.

Out riding, you pass Puffas, windcheaters, the odd hacking jacket, a variety of jerseys, anoraks, Australian stockman's coats with caped shoulders (very flash). My waxed jacket is part of me and my wardrobe. No matter that the wax is now patchy in places – the factory will do a rewax when things get desperate. It's perfect for riding, or almost. When it rains really hard, there is a little spot around the saddle pommel where the jacket rides up – because I've shoved the back over the saddle cantle to avoid sitting in water. This spot coincides with the top of the chaps where denim reappears, and of course this is rather uncomfortable as I end up with wet underwear.

What can you do? My answer is to carry waterproof trousers, rolled and slung across the back of my saddle in winter. They are a great insurance policy against a wet bum. The only trouble is they are a major kerfuffle to get into in the pouring rain. Imagine it. You are up on the Forest being torn to pieces by the wind and then it begins to rain. You think, 'Oh, hell; it'll pass.' And by the time you've realised that no, it's not going to pass, you are already getting damp in this awkward spot. So you turn for home and Callum, being a chancer by nature, thinks 'thank heavens for that' and gets a lot more active. His vote is not for slowing down and certainly not stopping.

Now you think, 'Do I get off and unsling the water-proof trousers in the wind and the rain while my horse does the foxtrot around me, just missing my toes time and again or do I wait to get to a more sheltered spot?' The sheltered spot always wins out. And by the time you are there, wetness has set in with a vengeance.

Now the question is, 'Do I still get off and into the wa-terproofs or just tough it out as we are on the way home?' – though wetness is going to be terminal by the time you reach sanctuary. You get off the horse. He, good chap, eats imme-diately, anything that is going, and you unstrap the trousers from behind the saddle. Now you have to get wet boots with spurs and leather chaps into these awkward flapping things, with elasticised tops and bottoms, and which the horse does not like anywhere near him. An undignified dance ensues.

You yank and pull and curse and finally get them on. Now you have turned into a gleaming green, shiny wet-look rustling thing, that the horse wants nowhere near him, least of all in the saddle. And your nether regions are cold and wet. This is when thoughts of golf or dog walking enter your mind, and how sensible the French are to like horse steak.

But you have not ridden for years to give up now; a remnant of expertise comes to your aid, as does a polo-mint and some native cunning. You get a foot in the stirrup, swing up and settle into a little swimming pool, custom designed for your bum. One wet bit says hello to another. You squelch home, disgustedly. No such thing as bad weather, Mr Wain-wright? You trusted to shank's pony rather than throw a leg across a horse. Sensible man!

But once geared up properly for the weather, there is a decided pleasure in heading out into the winter wildness. The Met Office is getting more accurate with its forecasts every year. I find I can pretty much rely on its predictions to know what part of the day is going to be wettest or most likely to be dry and ride out accordingly. And there are benefits to be found in riding in inclement weather, different from riding in the sun, but just as pleasurable. The very act of braving bad weather makes the heart beat faster, there is an edge to it, and some apprehension. But, as ever, once in the saddle, this concern fades as I enter the woods and the everyday comforts of my home slip into time past. Now it is the woods that offer sanctuary even as the wind bends the trees and some rain finds me. There is a sense of adventure and a self-regard for your grit in getting out there. The horse is likely to be more on his toes, and as you work to collect and balance him, there is a greater demand on your riding skills.

My reactions and instincts are on high alert for anything that will startle the horse; a falling branch, a leaping squirrel or deer. Now I am part of the weather – bathing in it, you might say. I ride beneath the cold bare trees, revealed in all their nakedness, their cloaks leafless, standing statuesque in nothing but mossy boots and a lingerie of ivy creepers.

I find myself once more standing amid the family of great beech trees in Five Hundred Acre Wood, before the fungus font decorating one of them. As I contemplate these giants, I feel the odd pulse of rain reach me and Callum, but it is just a sprinkle; I am warm and dry beneath my clothes.

I look at the trees and the thought comes to me that I am in the midst of water, both falling and rising. Within each wooden wall of the trees there are waterspouts rising vertically in their capillaries. I am a horseman in a watery world, with the vertical rising and falling of water all about me. I think of our son Dominic and his partner Stephanie at sea in their yacht, seeing waterspouts on the horizon, and I remind myself to tell them of my own beech-based waterspouts here on land. And, being a writer, my mind seeks a metaphor for my own life in this insight and of course it comes soon enough. Like the trees, I stand beneath a waterfall, not of rain, but of words, and like the trees, I take from this cascade what I need for sustenance, and within me rise my own words that become books made from the paper provided by trees. The trees and I are wood and flesh, but in some metaphysical way we are cousins at least, related by rain and writing, words and wood.

I look up through the treetops and the sky is a kaleidoscope of changing cloud shapes and tones, bringing light and dark to this forest dell and the path home that I choose.

And then we are home after an hour or two, and the sense of achievement is palpable, and the comforts of home the more intense for being hard-earned in the wet. Callum is dried off and rugged in his stable, his hay net full, and I feel I deserve my own meal and my drink and the right to relax and put my feet up. I reach for my laptop and start writing, because that is what I do. I write of wind and weather, rain and words, clothes and connections. This is all a gift of the weather, as is the buzz it brings with it and the words.

IN SEARCH OF A HORSE

Julian Roup

F or some years, Jan and I shared Traveller, our Irish Sports Horse, a bright chestnut-and-white skewbald, who we bought when he was seven; he is now approaching twenty.

This horse is the nearest thing there is to an equine saint. Not to say he is not capable of a good shy, and he can take a death hold on his bit and go like the clappers at the drop of a hat, but his heart is in the right place and his soul would not be out of place in a good priest.

But now he is getting a tad arthritic and has struggled with a number of ailments over the last three years. Jan continues to nurse him along through his issues. So we felt it was time that he had it easier and that a new horse would help take the strain off him.

I was going to turn 69 shortly, so my priority for the new horse was that he – a gelding is always my preference – be a good solid and reliable 'old man's horse', one that was a steady chap, and not too tall, making it easy to get off and back on for calls of nature and for the odd leg-stretch when tired, or when hips and knees creak.

We have had such good luck with purebred Irish Draughts like Dexter and Chancer, and Irish Sport Horses like Traveller, that this was the main focus of our attention. And, of course, he had to be sound, not a horse that was subject to lameness of any kind and seldom sick or sorry and with a kind temperament, as you want your horse to be a friend. And inevitably, not too expensive. Nor too young and flighty, nor too old – it's bad enough having an elderly rider. ('Speak for yourself!' says Jan). So a horse between five and ten years old would be ideal. You don't wish to give friends the opportunity to bet which one will croak first – horse or rider.

It did not sound like a tall order to me. I was not looking for a Badminton three-day eventer, nor a Grade A show jumper, nor a crack hunter, nor a top dressage horse. A good solid hack would do just fine. But as luck would have it, the task of finding this good 'un was more difficult than I might have imagined in my wildest dreams.

The first horse that took my and Jan's fancy was a lovely grey, a pure Irish Draught named Wish, based in Ireland. The description of him in Horse Quest sounded ideal and the videos confirmed the description. He looked and went like a real good egg. He seemed comfortable and reliable and friendly. The seller, a dealer who mostly sold Connemara ponies, even went so far on the video to show how you could duck right under his belly from one side to the other and he would not turn a hair. He was six years old and within our budget. The videos showed him jumping and riding in traffic. Just perfect!

But we are not fools. Sixty years of buying and selling horses have taught us caution and a thing or two. A horse can be drugged and made to look as though butter would not melt in his mouth.

Our opening shot was a telephone call to Ireland. The lady horse dealer sounded nice and straight and honest. She pointed out that Wish had a scar on his right knee, but her vet said it was a very old scar and did not in any way mean the horse was not 100 per cent sound. We said that was good to hear and that we would be getting a second opinion from a local vet that we would appoint for the job. No problem, said the seller, and indeed the horse passed his vetting with flying colours. Money changed hands and Wish headed for Sussex by ship and road trailer, with an overnight stay at a stable en route.

Wish arrived safe but not, it seemed, that sound. As Richard Wilkinson our horse guru led him off the box, he said he thought the horse was not going sound. And he seemed a bit smaller and more lightweight than he had looked in the pictures. More 16 hands than the 16.2hh described.

After a few days Richard saddled him up for a ride out and it was immediately evident the horse was in discomfort. We called in Rory, a brilliant locally based Irish vet who took

X-rays of the scarred knee. The result was a shock. There was long-term damage to the knee, which had been broken in a fall. We had been conned.

During the fortnight the horse was with us, his nature was also called into question. Katherine Seymour, an expert local rider, said that while she was mucking him out one day he reared up and struck out at her. A few days later, as I was grooming Wish, he reared up and struck out at me too. I left the stable quickly.

Now the problem became what to do. How to get Wish back to Ireland – and how to get our money back? Happily, there is a social media site called 'Dodgy Horse Dealers' which is the kiss of death to crooked horse dealers. No one wishes to get a mention on this site. A flurry of diplomatic emails was sent along with the X-ray images and the vet's report and the comment that we would hate to have to involve Dodgy Dealers. Wish returned to Ireland and we received our money back promptly. As the old adage has it, 'If wishes were horses, beggars would ride.' We had almost been beggared ourselves by a horse called Wish. Jan wanted to keep him. But Katherine whispered to her, 'You can't save them all…' To this day we wonder what became of this lovely, damaged horse.

After this catastrophe, which left us hundreds of pounds out of pocket with two vet's bills to pay and the transport to and from Ireland, we stopped looking for horses for at least a week. But the desire for a new horse is akin to heroin; once embarked on riding the dragon, it is not easy to dismount.

We charged up to a lovely farm in Yorkshire to see a flea-bitten grey gelding. He was a rather racy looking individual but was a lovely ride in the paddock and out on a hack. Trouble was he had cancerous sarcoids, which the owner had told us in advance, and was not 100 per cent sound, which he hadn't. But it had been a good drive and we spent a pleasant overnight stay in a nearby town whose only downside was the overwhelming stench of pig manure on the land nearby.

A bit crestfallen, we continued to scan Horse Quest,

Horse & Hound and various Irish Draught and Irish websites. We booked plane tickets for Ireland, thinking, despite our recent experience, that as this is where some of the best horses in the world come from, let us take ourselves off to this fabled land and go and see with our own eyes what was on offer.

From Dublin airport, we drove south in our hire car to the town of Kilkenny, where we spent a night, and the next morning drove further south to a small dealer's yard where there were two greys for sale. One was a stunning 17hh gelding that looked like a handful and the second a 16.1 hand chunky chap called Jimmy who I liked on sight. He gave us a fairly bumpy, short-striding ride in the paddock, but seemed like a good soul. Then it was down to Cork and a total waste of time at a beautiful country estate where the bay gelding we had come to see was rather unfortunately put together. We decided to make an offer on Jimmy, subject to a full vetting.

The vetting a week later, when we were back in Sussex, turned up a sarcoid and a wind problem. The Irish vet said neither would present a problem in a horse for hacking. Maybe not, but selling him on would not be easy if it came to that. We passed on Jimmy rather sadly.

We had greatly enjoyed our trip to Ireland. The craic was great as ever, the country lovely and the people could not have been more charming. But still no horse to show for our efforts.

A strange thing happens to you when horse hunting. It is bit like dating. You fall in and out of love rapidly, the highs are exhilarating and the lows a crash landing. It is exhausting when it extends over weeks and months, as our search did. You drive out in hope and anticipation and some trepidation about what you will be throwing your leg over, and come home crestfallen, bereft, more often than not. The horses are not at all as described, look nothing like their pictures, are green as grass, totally unschooled, and on occasion, vicious, wild and sometimes downright dangerous.

Throughout this time there was both a song and a descant playing in my head. The positive melody was this. 'Horse riding is your thing, how much longer do you think you have? It will bring you such pleasure and looking after it and riding it will keep you fit. Are you really ready for the sofa?' The descant went like this. 'It's not cheap to buy and will cost a lot to keep. This one you will have to do yourself and that means no more lie-ins. It means mucking out, grooming, riding in sunshine and showers, heat and cold. You will no longer be a free agent, able to use each day as it suits you. Instead, you will be a servant to your horse, not the other way round'. We had looked after our own horses for nearly three decades, so I knew what I was getting into.

One day the melody would sound loudest in my head, the next day the descant. And so it went, on and on.

We drove north once again to see another grey belonging to a hunt whipper-in, and this horse we both rather liked. A chunky 16.2hh Irish grey, useful over a ditch and very comfortable. Jan rode him in the paddock and he seemed distracted and nervy. The owner said his mare was in season, and this was the reason. We walked away.

Next, we made our way to a very reputable dealer in the Midlands, recommended by a high-profile hunting dealer in Northern Ireland, who had sent them a big chestnut to sell on.

My opening gambit to each new seller we met was: 'The old age home let me out early this morning to make the trip.' Nobody ever laughed. I could see them thinking, 'Oh God, the horse is going to kill this old fart!' We could also see it in the way they tacked up the horse and their nervous advice on what to do and what not to do. It took bottle to get on some of the beasts we looked at and both of us rode each one.

Today was no different. A young couple who ran this selling yard in the Midlands told us the horse had soured to jumping, but was a lovely hack if jumping was not my thing. I looked at the horse. He was a big athletic fellow, about 17.2 hands, but I was not that crazy about his head, which was plain in the extreme. He looked as if he'd had a hard life. I tried him in the paddock and thought he moved very well. I was once more warned about his jumping issues, but on one particular circuit of the arena we cut a corner and the horse thought I was heading for a jump in the middle. He dropped his shoulder and jinxed violently to the left and I nearly flew off to the right. Despite this, I liked him enough to ask if I could hack him up the nearby lane which I did without further incident. Jan rode him too and liked him. We left the decision hanging, saying to the sellers we'd have lunch in a pub and think it over.

It was a bit of a fraught lunch. The horse ticked a lot of boxes but with this jumping thing, what other issues might he have? And it was not love at first sight. If we took him, it would be more of an arranged marriage. In the end we decided we would take him on trial if the sellers agreed and have him vetted by our own vet at home. They agreed and a few days later, Red arrived.

I rode him out a couple of times, once just before the vetting. I was getting on with him very well and on this last ride found an extra gear. The horse lifted into that wonderful impulsion warmbloods have, collected and driving from behind. We trotted alongside the river at the valley bottom as if on clouds. There was no effort from me. He felt like a Rolls Royce. I knew then that I had found my horse, and what a horse!

The vet arrived a hour later and looked him over, put him through his paces on the ground, having him run up and down and turn tight circles. He listened to his heart, looked at his eyes and teeth and I felt things were going in the right direction. Then he started to work along Red's back and a look of concentration crossed his face. He had found something and was exploring it. After a minute or so he turned to me and asked, 'Have you ridden him out at all?' I said that both Jan and I had ridden him out on number of occasions and that he was a brilliant ride.

The vet shook his head and looked sad. His next words knocked the stuffing out of me. 'In all conscience, I can't let you get onto him again; his back is shot.'

That would explain his fear of jumping. This was a horse that had suffered a crashing fall out hunting and was living in pain. It said much for his good nature that he had carried us both so beautifully while suffering.

It was with a very heavy heart that we sent him back. The vet was adamant that there was no exercise regime or physio or operation that would fix this horse. The horse world is a brutal place at times.

Throughout this time, we made pilgrimages to East Grinstead to one of the best-known local dealers, Abbie Hart, accompanied by Katherine Seymour, who is a fund of expertise and also very good company. When horse hunting, you are lucky to have her in your corner. Over the months, we looked at a number of horses in this yard, becoming more and more embarrassed by our inability to commit. There was a stout 16.3hh bay Herbie, who seemed nice, but he was just too heavy-footed. There was Harry, an achingly beautiful chestnut, some 17hh, who looked and felt too sharp by half, and who I have no doubt would have caused me grief on a cold Ashdown morning. He had the look of eagles in his eye and carried himself like a prince. He kept trying to step or jump out of the dressage arena. If I was having trouble steering him in this enclosed space, I did not fancy my chances when out in the vast spaces of the Forest, when, no doubt, he would reach over from the co-pilot's chair and take command of the plane. I was having none of him. But oh, so beautiful. And between these two, there was a workmanlike grey mare, and one or two others with whom I did not click.

We drove up to Yorkshire again and tried a number of horses being sold by a partnership of two young men who were keen hunters. All their horses had something, but nothing clicked here either.

I next found a very nice stamp of horse in the Berkshire Downs, a bay gelding of about 16.3hh named George. He looked a good workman-like sort who could win a working hunter class, a good middleweight with a great depth of girth and a noble head.

I rode him in the paddock and liked him enough to try him up on the Downs on my own. He went so sweetly that once I had crossed a line of hills, I turned him for home and gave him his head and he galloped up that hill like a good chap. By the time I got back to the stables, Jan had caught me on video with a huge grin. The horse and I had clicked and Jan rode him and liked him too. We felt that we had finally found the one.

Rory, the Irish vet, went out to see him a few days later. He found that the horse had a massive heart murmur and he said I was lucky the horse had not dropped dead under me when galloping up that hill. Back to square one. The owner of the yard was embarrassed and said he had no idea his client's horse had a problem. Buyer beware!

We next looked at a chestnut gelding, a warmblood, in Kent close to home, near the Dartford Tunnel. He looked and felt a bit sharp. We decided against him.

The next day, somewhat depressed, I sat myself down on the couch with my MacBook, determined to turn something up and looked hard once more at Horse Quest. A big chestnut called Callum, a 10-year-old gelding based in Lincolnshire, jumped out at me. There were some nice pictures of him including one of him lying in his field basking in the sun. And there were two videos, one of him jumping and one of him working in a paddock. There was also a video of his rider getting off onto a mounting block, as he was so tall. He stood quietly, untethered, while she slithered down his side. By now, we had been at this lark for almost a year and were close to throwing in the towel. And this horse was a four-hour drive north. It would mean a full day of driving up and down.

I called the seller. She sounded nice. A young woman selling the horse for a farming couple who had owned him from the age of four. They had been using him as a hack around the farm, the mount of the husband, the less expert rider, who did not have much time to ride him. They were looking for a good home for the horse, and Charlie, the dealer, was a friend. Not a bad story, and a good start.

I told Jan and showed her the advert. She was lukewarm and said she thought I should go up alone, but in the end came along – in the game till the bitter end if needs be. It was a long journey with the weather closing in with heavy wind and rain. As we approached the farm, my usual butterflies started up. Another strange horse to ride, with who knew what result.

We got out of the car and met Charlotte and Ben, who walked us into the horse barn, and there stood Callum, a huge golden chestnut, a show hunter type with magnificent quarters, deep girth, a great head and neck, good shoulders and quality bone to his legs. Jan and I looked at each other for a split second and that look said it all; we'd finally found the right horse. He was magnificent. But how would he ride?

There was a thin cold rain borne on a biting wind, not a great day to try a new horse, and also the best kind of day, if you really want to know what the horse is capable of. He stood like a rock while I mounted and Charlotte, Ben and I rode out onto the farm through waist high grass at the edge of a grain crop. The horse felt sharp but not dangerous, and after a while settled into a good walk. We reached a long hill with a wide grassy ride running up it and I asked if I might give him a canter to the crest, thinking to myself this would be make or break. Callum rolled easily into a huge ground-covering canter, I rose in the stirrups and urged him on. He seemed in no rush and just cruised up the hill heading home. Calm and straight. No sudden deviations left or right. When I pulled him up on the top of the hill, I knew I had found my new horse and said as much to Charlotte and Ben who looked just a tad surprised but very pleased. Jan and I were the first to see him. Jan then rode him too and we were in agreement. He was the one, subject to vetting. Charlotte made us all a cup of tea and we sat by Callum's stable where he stood munching hay, belly deep in golden straw.

A week later we drove back up north to observe the vetting, which went without a hitch. The vet could not find anything to fault. We agreed to buy his tack and blankets too, and a few days later, just after my 69th birthday, he arrived, calm and happy, having travelled down very well, said the horse transporter.

We gave him a few days to settle in for his quarantine in the new stable yard, and finally the day came for a first ride on our own turf.

I tacked him up in his own bridle and his lovely deep dressage saddle, and we set off down the back hill. Callum felt as though he was ready to run a race and all the while screamed like a stallion. I thought that I had totally over-horsed myself. But other than the odd start at birds and squirrels that appeared suddenly, he did not put a foot wrong and after an hour of a few Ashdown hills we rode home on the rein buckle. It had taken us a year to find him, but it had been worth the wait. What a horse!

As I groomed him on our return and tucked him up for the night, my thoughts turned to all those many other horses we had seen, the many damaged horses, those with broken backs, compromised lungs and hearts and those gone in the legs. Horses who still tried for me despite the pain they must have been in. May they all find loving caring homes or a quick painless death. The price of horse riding is not only in the cost of the horse and its keep, it is paid for by the horses in pain and suffering. For those who object to hunting because of the cruelty to foxes I would say, add in the broken, damaged, wrecked horses. I've heard all the arguments that hunting is the making of a horse, will put lead in its pencil, teach it to look after itself and its rider. Maybe, but at what cost? If we humans do not take better care of our horses, then we must not be surprised when one day there is a law which outlaws riding as a cruel sport.

SPIRIT ANIMAL

Julian Roup

As I muck out Callum's stable this morning a rare, sweetly hesitant, shy sound stops me working and I stand and listen. Transfixed. It is the sound of a cuckoo close by in one of the trees surrounding the stable yard. My other African bird friend, like the swallow, but this long-haul traveller is a thief, a shyster, a murderer, a nest emptier, but lovely, oh so lovely. It is not the first cuckoo I have heard this heartbreak spring of 2020, but it is the closest, loudest, clearest. Work halted, I barely move or breathe, just listen. We've lost over half the cuckoos visiting Britain this last 20 years. They are becoming rare.

They come to us in early May out of the tropical rain-forest of the Congo, the very heart of Africa, one of the last homes of the last of the great apes, the gorilla. Their route to Britain takes them round the bulge of West Africa over river estuaries, then minarets and out over the Straits of Gibraltar, looking down on coasters and yachts, fast drug launches, refugee boats, oil tankers and container ships. And then through Spain, climbing high to cross the Pyrenees into France past monasteries and lonely wolf-haunted sheep farms, through France then and once more across a salt strait, the Channel, and home at last for the summer. Maybe this bird has been watching me cleaning the stable and has compared me to another big ape back in our mutual second home, Africa. It is enough romance, even for me.

I start lifting the shavings, winnowing out the drop-pings, filling the wheelbarrow, still listening. The cuckoo's song lasts for about two minutes and then the bird is gone, and I push the barrow to the muckheap, knowing I'm holding a sound-diamond in my head, turning each gleaming facet to repeat.

When I was still very young, six or seven years old, my parents took the family to the Kruger National Park in South Africa. We drove the 1,000 miles north from our home in

Cape Town, overnighting along the way, making it a two-day trip. The moment we entered the Park another energy filled the car, a watchfulness, a slight sense of danger. We were a small family, parents and three children in a car, alone in a primordial world filled with wild animals who called this place home. We were interlopers, and we were on our own.

We were lucky. We saw everything: majestic giraffes moving like cartoon characters; rhino who stood and stared; Cape buffalo; zebra; every kind of antelope including the herds of impala. These sleek, two-toned, chestnut-and-white animals appeared to move on springs which allowed them to form arabesques over the road at a height of six foot and more, effortlessly. And we saw lazy prides of lions, often lying in the dust of the road sunning themselves, sometimes in the long grass, heads just visible, scanning the bush.

And then, one morning, lions and impala performed a brief play, a tragedy, a dance that was part darkness, part light, part life, part death. We noticed two lionesses cross the road in that peculiar slinking motion cats have when hunting, torsos close to the ground, heads low. They disappeared into the bush to our left. A herd of impala then began filtering over the road, from right to left, looking agile and agitated and it soon became clear why. They were being herded from behind by a pride of lions. The buck came past faster and faster, leaping the road and now and then the bonnet of the car. Suddenly the two lionesses that had earlier moved across the road into the brush emerged amid the stream of impala and leaping up, caught one by the throat in mid-air. A bite and a shake of the lioness's head and it was all over. The bleeding impala was held down in the dust of the road as the pride converged on their dead prey and feasted right by our car. I don't remember being scared or horrified, but I do remember being electrified by the stalk and kill happening so close to us. The lithe beauty of the antelope, the electric energy of the lions, the blood in the dust and on the dead antelope's body, the blood on the mouths of the feasting lions, one of which looked straight into the car at us. Nature had delivered a spectacle right in front of us, the oldest in the world; the need to eat, to feed, to survive, and the death that it entails. It was as though a curtain had been briefly drawn back on our safe domestic reality to show us an older, ancient world. We spoke of it with wonder, for days afterwards. I remember my mother saying that nature was cruel.

Why do I think of antelope and deer as my spirit animal? Maybe it was the feeling of pity aroused by the sight of that kill in front of my eyes when I was so young. Maybe it was the rare sightings of Steenbok on the Cape Flats where I rode as a boy with my soul bruised from the hammering it took at school, where I was a very poor pupil. I'd see these animals always grazing singly amid the Port Jackson trees and it was a balm. I knew then that even as I sat trapped in a school desk beset by a world of worry, failure and pain, these animals were out there, miles from any human habitation, living their lives at peace, silently, quietly, with no need of a matriculation certificate or any need to understand the rules of rugby and cricket. I felt they were brothers and sisters, and so they have remained to this day.

For me, there is no difference between antelope and deer – but physiological differences there are. The most prominent difference is that male deer have antlers which they shed and grow every year, while antelope have horns that are permanent. Antelope belong to the family *Bovidae* (as do sheep, goat and cattle), while deer belong to the family *Cervidae*. I don't distinguish; I love them all.

At the age of 19, in the Army, doing my national service in the hot hell of Oudtshoorn's *veld*, there would be the occasional sighting, always distant, of an antelope and I'd know I was not alone; my tribe travelled with me, almost invisibly.

And when I reached Ashdown Forest in East Sussex in 1984, having left South Africa in 1980 to make a new home, I found myself surrounded by herds of deer, hundreds of them, in this former royal hunting ground. Roe deer are the only native deer on the Forest, I am told. They are strongly territorial, and so can regularly be seen in the same areas. The Ashdown Forest population increased after the great storm of

45

1987, which, with the loss of so many trees, restructured a great deal of the woodland, creating grassy glades and open rides. But the most common deer hereabouts are Fallow deer, with the odd sighting of a rare Sika or Muntjac deer. Occasionally I would spot a white Fallow deer, standing out clearly amid its brown brothers and sisters in the green fields.

These animals have no predators but man, and that largely by accident. Speeding cars take a terrible toll of them and there are signs on Ashdown Forest listing the number of animals killed each year. Now and then we will pass one, freshly killed by the wayside. It is a sight that pains me to the heart.

In autumn, the deep woods echo to the sound of stags belling. The roar is not that very different from a lion's roar and grunt. Once again, I find a sound bridge between my African boyhood and my adult life in Britain.

Twice, I had a close encounter with a stag. The first occurred when a stag caught its antlers in the electric fence around our horses' field, erected to prevent them breaking out. Instead of jumping the fence, which it could easily have done, this stag must have used his antlers to rip the electric fence wires out of his way as he grazed and became entangled in it more and more, being shocked by it all the while.

By the time I got to the field the stag was desperate, jumping wildly and thrashing, trying to escape. I ran to disconnect the fence at the battery and then ran for wire cutters, but I was too late. It died of a heart attack, according to the farmer I called to help me remove the carcass from the entanglement and then from the field. That was a bitter day.

And then there was an encounter that I still marvel at today. I was out riding early one morning in Five Hundred Acre Wood near my home. I was on a big dapple grey called Chancer who looked like a cloud himself, a dappled, water-carrying raincloud. We went carefully in the reduced visibility and suddenly he stopped. Planted hard, not moving but growing two or three hands higher, as horses do when electrified with fright or excitement. He quivered as he stood there, his neck a taut bow, ears sharply pricked at something I could not see in the dense fog. And slowly a white ghost moved out of the white towards us, a milk-white stag. It saw us and stopped, looked at us hard for a few long seconds and then whirled away back into the mist. As he leapt back into cloud cover, so did Chancer, and we whirled away ourselves.

Stags and deer haunt my dreams. And I know I am not alone.

Julian Roup

THE GREAT CIRCLE RIDE

Julian Roup

E very now and then, let's say every 10 years or so, a good long while anyway, there comes upon me a feeling, much like that beating in the heart of a swallow about to launch itself once more from Cape Town to Crowborough, a feeling that speaks to me quietly but insistently, which says, 'It's time, brother, time to do the "Great Circle Ride" again.'

When the call comes, it is always with a mix of excitement and a touch of apprehension, because while this is not remotely a journey to equal that of the swallow or indeed Jason in search of the Golden Fleece, or Columbus who found a 'new' world, in a smaller way it is no less daunting. To me anyway. I'm one of those who has to screw his reserve of courage to the sticking place.

I never answer the call immediately. I let it brew, think about it, brood on it. The ride will be a marking of my riding world's boundaries, a sort of beating of the bounds, a wolf marking his territory.

My usual riding grounds include Tilhill Forest and the area below the Horder Centre in Crowborough, the fabled Five Hundred Acre Wood, the stretch down to Poohsticks Bridge, across to the ancient thirteenth-century pub, The Hatch, then up the steep climb to Kidd's Hill and the heights of The Enchanted Place, and the Hollow on the Hill. Then across to King's Standing and the area that backs onto the Crow & Gate Pub on the A26 at Crowborough. South from there to the Garden of Eden Waterfall and the gallop up to Camp Hill Clump and then south once more to the pond and up to Friend's Clump, then across the road to Nutley between the cattle grids and the heights that command views of the South Downs. Then down one of the four paths in the southern part of the Forest that holds the Airman's Grave and descending further south to the lane called Cackle Street. And then east across the road to the village of Fairwarp and north, looping behind the Fairwarp tearoom and plant nursery. And from there, back across the road to the Nutley windmill, past Friend's Clump once more and down into the valley with its two stream crossings and up the hill to Pippingford Park. And if you and your horse have the energy, a loop that takes in the second World War emergency aircraft landing strip and across to the area close to Harold Macmillan's former home at Birch Grove and the clump of pines planted to honour the visit of President John F. Kennedy to Sussex on 29 June 1963. America's youthful and charismatic leader paid a flying visit to meet Prime Minister Harold Macmillan at his country house in Ashdown Forest.

This scimitar-shaped piece of countryside is my stamping ground, my riding country.

To link the point of the sword to its pommel, you must tackle the road from Wych Cross traffic lights along the ridgeway past the Ashdown Forest HQ and the entrances to the Ashdown Park Hotel, and then through the woods, skirting The Hatch and then down into the splash and up Kidd's Hill and home to Crowborough. Or one can do that ride the other way round, which I prefer. It is a ride that can be done in a brisk three hours on a fit horse, some 12 to 15 miles, I guess.

I never approach this ride lightly, as I dislike any kind of roadwork that places horses on roads used by motor traffic. Horses are unreliable at times and perfectly capable of shying into the path of an oncoming car or one that approaches from behind, if the horse thinks there is a lion in the woods next to the road. Many a motorist blithely believe horses run on rails, much like trains, and don't understand the athleticism that will move a horse and rider suddenly, unexpectedly, 30 foot sideways in the blink of an eye. And navigating through the four-way traffic light junction at Wych Cross takes nerve for any horse and rider.

So the 'Great Circle Ride' takes a modicum of courage and some resolve, which gives me a great sense of satisfaction once safely completed. I imagine Columbus felt the same way on his arrival back at the Spanish Court. You feel something like the return of the conquering hero. The horse just feels knackered, I expect.

As you ride the Forest, you inhabit two worlds, the real, living, breathing one created by nature; and if you are a reader or love art the second Forest all about you, the one created by the writers and artists who lived and worked here and loved the forest.

For example, the interior design for Ashdown Forest is by William Morris, who by no small coincidence has his fingerprints and wallpapers all over Standen House, in East Grinstead, now a National Trust property. As I ride over his carpets of leaves – a star spangled banner of white, red, maroon, orange, yellow, green, brown, and black – I cannot help but pity the celebrities on the red monotony of Hollywood Oscar and Cannes Film Festival carpeting.

And the Forest 'wallpaper' is also by this genius, holly, honeysuckle, beech, oak and silver birch erupting from the ferns and bracken, wild berries and dog rose hips a counterpoint to the green palette.

William Morris is remembered as a visionary who spearheaded the Arts and Crafts movement and inspired generations of artists and designers. He was a revolutionary force in Victorian Britain. His most famous maxim lives on – 'Have nothing in your houses that you do not know to be useful or believe to be beautiful' – and his influence can still be seen today in English homes and design. The Forest is no different and I have no doubt that it influenced his work.

After studying theology at Oxford, Morris trained as an architect and became close friends with Pre-Raphaelite artists Dante Gabriel Rossetti and Edward Burne-Jones, who influenced him greatly too. They also can be found here on the Forest if one looks closely enough into the placid streams and the statuesque woods.

This place is not just an artist's inspiration, it is also a literary landscape, with A.A. Milne's Pooh Bear and friends, Sir Arthur Conan Doyle's Sherlock Holmes, and the work of the two great poets, the Irishman W.B. Yeats and the brash American Ezra Pound, who spent three winters at Stone Cottage, near The Hatch Inn at Coleman's Hatch. Yeats, at 48, was 20 years older than his companion, and Pound later recalled that in the winter of 1913-14 Yeats had not been an easy companion, making a fuss over a number of things including not wanting hot ham for his dinner – the food of peasants, said Yeats. It's a strange and wonderful thing to think of these two geniuses on the Forest, and my horse's hooves marking the trails they would have walked.

For me, one of the great surprises of Ashdown Forest, when I first arrived here 40 years ago as a would-be writer, was its connection with these two literary giants of the twentieth century. For me, Yeats's poem *The Lake Isle of Innisfree*, speaks of my hideaway in this landscape. As I tramped London's grey streets to earn a crust, these words would echo through my mind.

> 'I will arise and go now, and go to Innisfree,
> And a small cabin build there, of clay and wattles made:
> Nine bean-rows will I have there, a hive for the honey-bee;
> And live alone in the bee-loud glade.
> And I shall have some peace there, for peace comes dropping slow,
> Dropping from the veils of the morning to where the cricket sings;
> There midnight's all a glimmer, and noon a purple glow,
> And evening full of the linnet's wings.
> I will arise and go now, for always night and day
> I hear lake water lapping with low sounds by the shore;
> While I stand on the roadway, or on the pavements grey,
> I hear it in the deep heart's core.'

An article from the *New York Times* states:

> 'Ezra Pound recalls sitting in the second floor of Stone

Cottage and hearing Yeats chant his poetry in the room below – the chimney carried the Irish poet's brogue from fireplace to fireplace. When Pound wrote these lines in the *Pisan Cantos* at the end of World War II, he looked back to those Stone Cottage years as an idyllic time 'before the world was given over to wars.'

'The situation at Stone Cottage is unmatched in literary history: two of the greatest poets of the 20th century – and two poets so different in temperament – living in excruciatingly close quarters for months at a time. The idea was that Pound would serve as Yeats's secretary, and that both poets, freed from the obligations of literary life in London, would have the time and solitude to pursue their projects without interruption. "When breakfast was over, they would set to work as if life depended on it," recalled Alice Welfare, their housekeeper. "'Don't disturb him,' Mr. Pound used to say, if I wanted to dust, and Mr. Yeats would be humming over his poetry to himself in the little room." After supper, the poets would walk across the heath to the local inn for cider. "At night," wrote Yeats, "when the clouds are not too dark and heavy, the great heath is beautiful with a beauty that is not distracting. One comes in full of thoughts. When I am in the country like this, I find that life grows more and more exciting till at last one is wretched, when one goes back to London."'

All of this I found in Ashdown Forest when I first arrived from South Africa in 1980. Is it any wonder that the place inhabits my heart?

So thinking of my Great Circle Ride, timing is all – autumn or winter are best for this mini-Odyssey, thus an early start is made, to miss the rush hour traffic at Wych Cross.

The chosen day dawns misty but promises clear skies later. says the Met Office, crisp and clear. Just perfect. I feed Callum, who makes his usual terrifying face with ears laid back, which means 'Gimme the food and be quick about it mate' – and as he eats, I muck out his stable. He will want a good deep woodshavings bed tonight. I give him a thorough grooming and he closes his eyes and drops his head, blissed out; he is nothing if not tactile, and loves the brushes on his gleaming chestnut coat. I tack up more carefully than usual. It is going to be a long ride and we want no chafing.

I mount and as usual a deep satisfaction sinks into me. I'm home in the saddle once more. Callum steps out briskly into the morning, ready for the day, fit after an autumn of steady hacking around five to ten miles a day, the summer grass fat all muscle now. And his mood lifts mine too. From Crowborough we drop down the hill into Tilhill Forest, the army camp to our left, cross the two bridges over the streams that feed the lake to our right and head up, up, up, the long hill with the valley pasture of Ashdown Forest Riding Centre on our left and King's Standing commanding the southern skyline beyond.

We cross the road and are on the Forest proper now. I take the most direct path across the heathland to the car park atop Kidd's Hill and then we begin the steep descent to the splash at the bottom. Callum strides out like a good 'un. The road rising towards The Hatch Inn is almost traffic-free. It is early enough for us to have the road to ourselves, with perhaps just one or two pilots rushing off to Gatwick.

We gladly leave the road with a sharp left just before the pub and once more head into the woods where our first sighting of deer greets us. They are not too fussed and move away in a leisurely manner.

I feel a slight rising of tension, for I know ahead lies the mile-long ridge road, potentially our nemesis. It just takes one idiot driver, or a rattly truck, or Callum taking fright at something in the roadside bushes and our ride could end in a most unfortunate way. But danger faced and stared down brings its own reward of endorphin rush.

The big horse is just exercised enough by now that he is not looking for trouble or feeling like high jinks, and he trots like a metronome dead straight past the Ashdown Forest HQ and on to the garden centre at the Wych Cross traffic lights. The two or three cars that pass us slow down and give us a wide berth. I give them a wave and touch my hat by way of thanks. As we go, I sing an Afrikaans lullaby to the horse, whose ears flick back and forth, recognising the song which I first sang to him on the day he arrived, 18 months ago. On our first ride that day he had felt like an unexploded bomb. The song works its magic once more and Callum trots on, dead straight, his hooves clip-clopping on the tarmac road.

There is traffic awaiting us at the lights, at all four stops. I pull Callum up and I see that we are an object of interest to all the car drivers waiting there. They are aware of us, which is a good start. I am behind a small white van and a big black 4x4 glides up behind us. Callum stands firm. The lights change in our favour and we make a diagonal crossing briskly, the cars opposite giving us room and right of way. Callum looks at the lights askance and gives one huge truck a quizzical wary look, but he keeps going, feeling my legs hard on his sides and the reins indicating our direction of travel, into the brush chop-chop! And then we are through. Now we can relax on the long grass ride alongside the Forest Row to Nutley road. I breathe deep, check my girths and chill. Callum swings along, his ground-devouring walk making light of the going. I lift him into a canter and all feels right in the world.

We cross the road and drop down to the stables nearby to visit Traveller. He seems happy to see us. The visit gives me a chance to dismount and water Callum, to check my saddle and to stretch my legs.

After a break of half an hour, we are on our way again, dropping down to the wooden bridge across the stream, and then up the steep haul past the back of the Nutley windmill to Friend's Clump, with its views all around the points of the compass, the place busy with morning walkers.

I check the time. We've been gone two and a half hours, moving at a steady walk and trot, with short canters. The break leaves Callum feeling good and he is on the bit, still moving forward eagerly. We pass the pond, greet some walkers and then head up to Camp Hill Clump where I dismount on the bench and give the horse another chance to blow. Now we are on the home run and going slow and easy, an hour will see us back safe.

Soon enough we find ourselves recrossing the road and dropping down the hill past Ashdown Forest Riding Centre once more.

The trick is to pace your horse, and pace yourself. I stop now in the wood cover for a pee on one of the natural earthen mounds, like train station platforms, which run alongside the path through this wood; they facilitate an easy dismount and remount from a 17hh horse. There are regular places like this that I use through the Forest maze, which must make the foxes, badgers and deer scurry swiftly on, smelling my marker. The elevation these earth tables provide allow me to keep a sharp eye out for walkers and riders – one would not want to frighten either horse or rider with the untoward sight of an old man taking a pee. Callum is a philosopher horse, and he takes it all in his stride, using the opportunity to graze.

I remount and down the hill we go. Callum knows it's the home run now and his walk is the fastest of the ride, despite the distance covered. We cross the two bridges at the bottom of the hill and then there is just the last half-mile up the home hill to the stables. Once more I've done the Great Circle Ride and the sense of achievement at the age of 70 makes me happy. And Callum is just happy to be home.

SNOW ON ASHDOWN

Julian Roup

S now is not a problem we faced in South Africa. So to find ourselves housebound in our cottage on Ashdown Forest for the first time was exciting, to say the least.

When buying our home in 1984, we considered many things, but snow did not feature large in our calculations. The place had stood unsold for a year until we came along – it was just too remote for most people, though in a car it was just ten minutes to the high street. I should have known that at almost 1,000 foot of elevation, any snow in the South East of England would lie here the longest, and with no snow ploughs to clear the dead-end country lane we live on, we could well be snowed in for a while. And so it has proved.

It's not often that we get snow, but we've had snow as late as May and as early as November. There is no second-guessing the weather. Snow comes as a gift, its pristine beauty a miracle. Here on Ashdown, it blankets the vast spaces and transforms the landscape into something almost Alpine.

One needs a few things when the snow flies here. Enough oil in the central heating tank, gas for the hob, a generator in the event that the electricity fails, as it has done regularly for 37 years, and ideally a 4X4 to get up and down the steep lane to the A26 into Crowborough. It can be a long haul until the thaw frees us.

The beauty of it is that everything stops and silence reigns. Outside at any rate. With children and dogs and cats inside the house, it was not that silent. Outside, at the top of the garden, the horses had things rather more peaceful.

Snow and storms make you realise how fragile our lives can be and how dependent we've become on modern technology. Christmas 2017 was a case in point. Snow held off, but wild weather brought us a five-day power cut. And we had long ago sold our last generator, finding them inevitably not working after a year or three of not being required, the diesel turned to gel.

But our practical son, Dominic, was home for the holiday, and as the lights went out and the heating too and no chance of a hot shower, he stoked the wood burning stove and made candle candelabras out of tree branches. The cottage had never looked more festive. But Christmas dinner was going to be a challenge. We'd opted for a duck and though the gas hob was working, neither of the electric ovens were in action. How to cook it?

But necessity is the mother of invention. I decided that I would roast the duck in the woodburning stove. On Christmas morning I sent Jan and Dom for a good long country walk and set to in the kitchen at noon. I made sure that the wood stove in the living room was not too hot and had a good bed of coals. I placed the duck on a trivet inside and closed the doors. Back in the kitchen I peeled potatoes and prepped the other veg. Suddenly a burning smell reached me and I dashed through to the living room to check on the duck, which was a ball of flame, looking more like a blazing comet than any fowl.

I leant down and pulled open the doors of the woodstove. The fresh oxygen caused a mini fire storm that singed my eyebrows, but using two kitchen cloths, I managed to wrestle the burning duck out onto the stone plinth in front of the woodburner. What to do with this burnt offering? A veg-only Christmas did not appeal. I took the duck through to the kitchen and scraped away at its most blackened parts until it just looked badly singed, then returned it to the woodstove, leaving the doors open this time and the coals much reduced.

By the time Jan and Dom returned from their walk I had a great orange-brandy sauce to cover the duck, which had cooked through with no further excitements.

Munching Christmas dinner contentedly in the candlelight after their walk, they praised the 'lovely smoky flavour of the duck, complemented so well by the orange brandy sauce.' I accepted the comment graciously and said nothing till much later in the holiday week when they asked what had happened to my eyebrows. That burnt duck has become part of our family history and Christmas storytelling. And we relish it more and more with each telling.

A few days on without showers we were all beginning to smell rather Gorgonzola-like. Those neighbours who still had power came to the rescue with offers of showers which we accepted gratefully. Clean and warm once more by the wood fire, the sense of living a kind of frontier life made it all worth the effort. That wild, candlelit Christmas lives on in our memories as one of the best. And looking into the mirror each time I shave I see my regrown eyebrows once more in place and the smell and taste of smoky duck comes to mind.

Lying as high as Crowborough does, here in the south east corner of England, the snow has a multiplier effect. It is pretty, yes, it brings a blessed silence, yes, but it makes getting around tricky as hell. I remember driving a Saab that because of its weight, would continue to slip down the Beacon Road as the traffic lights turned red, and if there was a car in front of me all I could do was to turn the car's tyres into the pavement edge and that would stop me finally.

Coming home from work in London one night, my train pulled into Gatwick just as the snow started to fly. At the time I was driving one of the many Subaru Legacy Outbacks I have owned over the years, each of which I bought cheaply at around 90,000 miles, knowing they would be good for another 50,000 miles at least. With their reliable engines, permanent 4x4 drive and their relatively light weight, they would get me anywhere I needed to go in the snow.

On this night, I was blocked from reaching home by a jack-knifed truck and trailer on the steep hill down into Nutley. I did a U-turn and at the Wych Cross lights turned right and drove the ridgeway past the Ashdown Forest Centre, then stupidly tried my luck on steep Kidd's Hill, but halfway up the car began to fishtail, so gingerly I turned and slowly retraced my way past The Hatch, heading for the A26 Tunbridge Wells road. All went well until another jack-knifed truck blocked the A26 near Boars Head. I managed to cross the central reservation in my trusty Subaru and got into Crowborough via Jarvis Brook and the Green by the Church and then down the A26 into Fielden Lane, and finally home.

As I pulled into the drive my affection for that car rose in me and I gave it a pat and said, 'Well done!' Funny how inanimate steel can take on such a personality when you are up against the weather and it brings you safely through. I loved that car.

The old Subaru was also my partner in hauling the kids on sleds up our lane and down Fielden Road to toboggan on the Beacon Golf Course hill.

The snow, however, represented a major challenge in getting the horses exercised. It was no joke having big active Irish Draughts stable-bound for days on end, with just a small paddock for them to have a buck and kick in. One icy day, Jan took my horse Chancer out with Richard Wilkinson, our horse guru, riding her 17.2 hand horse Dexter, who had recently got above himself. They got out of our drive safely enough, but just before turning down into the woods Dexter went down sideways like a felled ox on the icy road, though Richard managed to throw himself clear, landing on his feet with balletic style. Snow, ice and horses do not mix easily.

It never ceases to amaze me, watching cowboy films where the horses carry their riders safely through waist-high snowdrifts. I still don't understand how they do that, given the way that snow will compact in a horse's shoes.

How the deer survive such bitter weather is beyond me. The fox and badger have warm lairs well below ground and company to snuggle up to in their bracken blankets. The squirrels have oak-framed homes and the birds have feathered nests. The deer are on their own at ground level in the snow.

During my years of commuting for work from Gatwick to London and later from Tunbridge Wells into London, the arrival of snow was a major headache before computers made working from home a possibility. The regular message that no trains were running and there was no way to get into work as the authorities were advising drivers to stay off the roads, was stress inducing. But once you accepted the inevitable, the silence of the landscape and the peace always brought its own reward, a great sense of gratitude that we had the good fortune to live on the Forest amid such beauty.

When the snow flies on Ashdown Forest, time slows, and the everyday demands of the busy workaday world ebb away. We return to a much older way of living, keeping warm, keeping fed, staying safe. Each step out of the house is a step into beauty but also into possible danger. Broken arms and legs and hips beckon on the black ice. I move cautiously, the mind in the now, the present, focused. After some days of this, I inevitably feel calmer and with it comes the deep satisfaction of managing despite the challenges. Hauling in wood for the fire, cooking, reading, eating, sleeping. The rhythm of the days is one our forebears would have known.

Outside, there is silence. It is utterly still but for the call of an owl in the dark and the soft patter of snow falling from wind lifted branches.

Julian Roup

THE WEEPING WOOD

Julian Roup

W e ride out of the stable yard into thick fog which clothes the whole of Ashdown Forest. It had been the coldest night of the winter thus far, 7 December 2020, the bitter end of the Covid-19 blighted year.

It has not been all bad. I've had a book out of it, and friendships deepened by daily WhatsApp conversations. There has been enough work to keep my mind active and there has been riding, miles and hours of riding, on average two hours and eight or ten miles most days. And I have new riding companions, a bay gelding named Finch and his rider, Zoe, who wants to learn the Forest trails.

I give Callum his head and he chooses to go south downhill to the lake at the bottom of the valley. I turn him right above the lake and we head west along the stream, turn north at the dogleg and trot the half mile to the bridge across the stream, which is also a way home up the back hill, but I keep him headed north along the path by the stream, through the gate and then a canter up a steep grassy hill to take the edge off him. He settles to it with a will and the hill flows beneath us like an earthen stream.

Quietly, we move through the fog, stillness all around us, no hint of a breeze in what can be a windy Forest. The trees stand tall in silent communication with each other, telegraphing our progress ahead on fungal lines below ground as we move among them. We stop to listen. Silence but for a faint hum of a car passing on the road through the Forest.

The mud beneath Callum's hooves is mulchy with the heavy autumn leaf fall, now turning into fresh earth. Here and there a squirrel moves, but no birds sing. It is eerie. But the smell of the wood, magnified by the damp of the fog, makes its own chorus in my nose, a mix of wet wood and earth with a hint of smoke.

Riding in a wood, a mood-bedevilled man is given the constant pleasure of choice, as paths offer height or depth, the points of the compass, light or dark, openness or overgrowth. I know where I am going, but the wood gives me options. The journey is never the same twice, always a different wood, like stepping into a river, never the same water.

Like the horse I am alert, living fully in the moment. My body, like his, moves as we traverse the landscape that speaks through us in the movements it demands. Our task is to move safely, not to slip in the icy wet, stay on the level, not allow tilted parts of the path to cause the horse's legs to slip from under him. It is a bit like driving a car on a skidpan.

We come to a gently rising path that has a gravel underlay with grass in the middle that has not been worn down by Land Rovers or logging equipment and this gives us a chance to change gear, lifting into a slow drumroll hand canter, collected, collected, collected. My helmeted head on this 17 hand horse sits ten feet off the ground as we roll up the incline. Callum's ears, eyes and nose scan the path ahead for danger which might demand a change of pace, a violent shy or a desperate gallop to avoid a predator. I know just what he is thinking and grip his sides with my thighs and calves, signalling my presence to him, telling him he is not alone. And giving myself a better chance of staying with him should he decide on evasive action. But his motion is steady and we flow uphill.

The beech trees gleam wet with the fog this morning and the rain that came in the night, and the diffused foggy light makes each tree its own drama, each a separate figure in this landscape.

We stop and listen once more for any sound of a land agent or gamekeeper's vehicle. But there is just deep silence and we move on.

On the final leg of this Forest ride, before turning downhill and home, we come to a grassy area mixed with winter-brown bracken and a little copse standing all on its own. Zoe and her horse Finch stop and she points to the copse. I pull Callum up as I can suddenly hear the soft patter of rain. Yet we stay dry despite the sound. Looking into the copse, I see the answer, the faintest breeze is moving the trees just enough to cause the night-collected rain on the leaves to shiver the water off and as it falls gently, it patters within the copse, which seems to be weeping.

The horses, Zoe and I stand rapt, observing this strange and wonderful phenomenon, a wood weeping, while we stand below a dry sky. We are in a magic kingdom, where a wood weeps in a silent mist.

Does it weep for joy or sadness? I will never know, but my thoughts bring to mind the 75,000 Covid-19 dead, enough to fill a giant sports stadium. And for me that wood weeps a sad threnody of remorse for lives lost, lives cut short. The water-music, a wood's echo of the countless tears that have fallen in this benighted island, this past nine months.

The breeze must have picked up, for suddenly I feel drops of water on my own cheeks.

Julian Roup

WINTER-FLOWERING CHERRY

Julian Roup

T here is a winter flowering cherry in our garden that commands views across Ashdown Forest to Kings Standing and the cherry gives me hope that the winter of my life, now well upon me at the age of 70, might yet produce some late blossom.

Each time I saddle Callum and ride out into the Forest, I am aware that this could be my last ride. Each ride therefore has a bittersweet, elegiac quality that adds to my pleasure but also sharpens the edge of apprehension.

I have been riding now for 65 years, ever since I got onto my first pony Duke at the age of six, and he ran away with me down Bloubergstrand beach near Cape Town. I fell off, hitting my head on one of the red brown rock formations that are found along that stretch of coast. I was concussed and was taken to Groote Schuur Hospital for a check-up. Happily, no harm was done.

The next day I was back riding Duke and after a week or two of practice, was able to take control of the pony properly and start to explore a wider world than I had known until then. It was an inauspicious start to a lifetime of riding, and looking back now, I am surprised that my mother allowed me back onto Duke. My father, who had been an accomplished rider in his youth, must have persuaded her that I would be fine, and that getting back up after a fall was character-building.

Now that my riding days are almost past, I value my relationship with horses almost more than at any other time of my life. I've had Callum for some 18 months now, and I hope he sees me through until my 80th birthday if I am spared. He is an inappropriate 'old man's horse' as he is a highly-strung warmblood, half Oldenburg, half Irish Sport Horse, and he has his moments. But we rub along together and the bond between us grows ever stronger. Yesterday for the first time he allowed me to approach him while he was lying down in his stable to stroke his head and neck.

When not whirling round to escape imagined horrors in the woods – doing an ice-skating style 'triple Lutz' to perfection – he is in many ways very laid back and will allow me to stop him under overhanging branches blocking our path, standing quiet while I break them off to clear our way. He will munch on leaves all the while. So all my rides have markers of our passing, broken branches that signal that a tall rider on a tall horse has been this way.

My riding country, Ashdown Forest, is a remnant of the primordial Forest of Anderida that covered southern England in dense, virtually impenetrable tree cover – oak, ash, beech, chestnut, birch, holly, yew and elm – for thousands of years, until people made clearings amid the woods, and later built a navy from its oaks and smelted iron ore, fuelled by burning Forest trees.

As Callum and I pass silently on our way we cover ground that has been hunted for millennia, this place of deer, wild boar, wolf, bear and badger.

I see them clearly in my mind's eye as we traverse the same landscapes, men, women and children dressed in skins and furs, carrying spears, bows and arrows, and the implements needed to cook. Hunter-gatherers, the Forest's first human occupants, arrived 40,000 years ago when the ice retreated north.

Back at the DIY stable yard where I keep Callum, there are 25 women riders and a small number of men. There are always more women than men in most stable yards. I am not sure why this is. Women love the beauty of horses and seem more able to negotiate their relationship with these animals. And a woman on a horse will go to places in the Forest where she may hesitate to go on foot. Horses are great getaway vehicles.

Men, on the other hand, I suspect, more generally, simply wish to be obeyed and do not take kindly to being bucked off and dumped on the ground. Or being kicked or bitten. The world of horses can be a harsh one, a place with a pecking order for the horses as much as the riders, and it is as well to know your place. It can be and often is a place of danger and injury and death, mostly for the horses but for the riders too, on occasion.

Recently the top rider in the yard, a three-day-eventer, who rides for England, had a bad fall at a practice jump and lost her spleen as a result. Yesterday, a woman out hacking in the woods was thrown by her horse and was concussed. The week before, a 26-year-old horse was put down, as they say when a horse is shot. It had started to collapse, as age caught up with it. Life and death are on intimate terms in the world of horses. It has always been this way, and in my six decades of riding I have seen much injury and some death. I am a walking roadmap of horse-inflicted injury. My knees are shot after multiple arthroscopies, the result of a horse rearing up and falling over backwards onto me when I was twenty. My hands, shoulders and elbows are arthritic from a lifetime of reining in over-eager horses.

Even as I ride into my dreamtime in the woods, a sense of danger rides with me every step of the way. It was ever thus, but as I have grown older and my vulnerability is more apparent to me – I won't bounce if thrown, as once I did – I have become more cautious.

This sense keeps me rigorously in the present, which is no bad place to be when you've lived as long as I have and have many regrets and failures to ponder from the past. The future does not hold too much appeal either. The present is the best place to be at the age of seventy. And I am not alone, so often the fate of the elderly, when my horse friend Callum is with me.

What sort of late flowering might I hope for or expect at this age? I am not a flowering cherry. But there are tantalising things afoot. Not least the beauty I am surrounded by, in nature, in horses and in the women riders who share this love of horses with me.

Recently, I have been showing Zoe some of my riding country, as she does not know the area well and asked to accompany me. We have ranged far and wide, and it has given me great pleasure to share some of my secret rides with her. A few days ago, we gave the horses their heads up the long steep hill that rises from the valley floor to Camp Hill Clump and they ate that hill as though inhaling it, fairly tearing up its grassy gallop. At the top we pulled up and my young companion said: 'You are like no other 70-year-old that I know!' I barely had a second to digest the compliment when a woman standing nearby, holding her dog, piped up: 'Don't tell him that! It's exactly what he wants to hear!' I could only wonder what life had given her to elicit that response.

Saffron, another riding friend, organised a surprise book-signing for me in the indoor riding school, which caught me totally on the hop. I had to steady the pen as I wrote inscriptions, almost overcome by emotion. She had bought my book for friends as Christmas gifts and they needed dedications. All this, two days before Christmas with all the organisation that demands. Yet she had arranged posters, a table bearing my books, a pen, and a cut-glass decanter of sloe gin. And an African touch, a leopard-skin print cloth thrown over the chair. I did my best, but all this kindness threatened to unman me.

Yesterday, Katie, another of my stable neighbours, whose horse Mickey stands alongside Callum, told me that she and some others now refer to themselves as 'Julian's Girls'. I did not know what to say. It was said teasingly but was meant kindly I hope, and I felt flattered. There is no fool like an old fool. A bit like bringing a burnt-out sparkler to a fireworks party. But there it is – a very late winter-flowering cherry. I thought I heard a muffled horse laugh from Callum's stable but when I looked over the door, he was straight-faced, keeping his own counsel. Maybe just as well.

WHEN NATURE CALLS

Julian Roup

G etting old is a terrible thing. There is very little to recommend it. I say this with all the authority of my 70 years toiling in this benighted vineyard, plus a bladder that refuses to empty itself completely. Getting old is indeed not for sissies.

Take horse riding on Ashdown Forest. Gone, long gone, are the days when I would have a pee at home and be gone for half the day before needing to pee again. Not so now. I still have a pee at home, knowing full well I will need to pee again in the next two to three hours. Drinking a *lot* of coffee does not help of course, but I'd rather wrestle with urination than give up the bean of wakefulness.

Ashdown of course is a 'pee-ers' paradise. There is always a gorse bush, a tree, or a whole wood to nip into for a bit of quick bladder relief. Oh, the pleasure of that and the renewed vigour it lends to your walk or ride; to be bloody empty for a while is bliss.

But as you get older, the call of nature comes more frequently and more insistently and you can be caught short on the Forest, where there are plenty of wide open spaces with little or sparse cover.

When riding out in my younger days, it was no problem to pop off the horse and have a pee next to the horse while he grazed. Horses are not prudes. But life catches up with you and it weakens your muscles and joints as well as your back and bladder. And you find yourself desperate to pee, but facing the seemingly Herculean task of remounting. There is a shame-inducing solution, and if I share this with you don't judge me too harshly, there are worse crimes in the world. If you are a man, the possessor of a penis anyway, you are free to rise in your stirrups and pee from the horse's back. I've done it many a time, when I simply could not be bothered to dismount off a tall horse – and all my horses have been tall. The horse, it must be said, does not object. He just wants to graze. So you pee as far from his grazing area as you can.

Be careful, though, that he does not spook while you are about this aerial display. It is no joke to find yourself being tanked off with while a penis is not safely encased behind a zip. People have gone to prison for less.

So, having cast a sharp eye around for anything that will spook the horse, you can release the pent-up urine in a bright shining arc and be done with it and ride on. Not so now. Not at seventy. The days of bright shining arcs are long past. The mechanism that enables you to let rip like a fire-hose is kaput, gone, *finito*.

The picture of an old man on a runaway horse, penis in the wind, is enough to startle the most robust woman walker. It's probably illegal. And if you try to stop to apologise, it only compounds the offence. Keep galloping, lad, until the safety of a wood is reached, then pull up and tuck the offending article away, even as you blush with shame. And don't even think of riding back to the lady in question to apologise. She has in any case run for her life back to her car and will probably never again venture out onto Ashdown's hallowed acres.

As ever with me, whatever the subject, it never takes long for my thoughts to slip 6,000 miles south to my boyhood home in South Africa. For there, too, there is a shame-inducing story involving the need to pee.

Imagine the scene: it is night on the Highveld and bitterly cold. The stars of the Milky Way gleam overhead above the little town of Potchefstroom. All around sleep thousands of lads out on army manoeuvres. They lie encased in five layers of clothing, snuggled deep within their sleeping bags, trying to keep warm and get some sleep. Outside, the starlight gleams on the tin 'lilies', the metal urination funnels erected outside each tent. They are useful implements, as they help you avoid the necessity of a long walk to the improvised long-drop toilets, hidden behind sacking in each quarter of the camp.

Now a sleepy boy edges out of his tent, needing a pee.

He is still half asleep as he unbuttons his overalls and his tracksuit to reach for his penis and he pops it unthinking onto the rim of the 'lily' and lets rip. Being young, it's over in seconds and he reaches for his penis to return it to the warmth of his clothes, but disaster has struck. It is frozen to the ice cold metal. He tugs gently at first and then frantically. There is no way the metal is letting go.

And now, frightened, he shouts for his friend to help. *'Koos, kom help my, my piel is vas aan die lily!'* 'Koos, come and help me, my dick is stuck to the lily!'

Minutes go by and frostbite is setting into his penis. Thoughts of possible amputation, of gangrene, cross his mind and he shouts once more for help. Eventually, Koos arrives, quite often with a gang of others interested to observe the coming operation and to give advice – literally to take the piss.

Koos fumbles for his own penis and being careful to avoid any contact with the tin lily lets rips all over his friend's dick. The warm urine works its magic and his friend is released from the icy clutches of the lily. All the onlookers cheer. The lads return to their sleeping bags, making mental note to avoid the same fate.

The next morning, over a breakfast of ice-cold fried eggs with blue yolks, congealed bacon and slices of bread with thin coffee, the victim of the night is teased. They say he tried to rape the lily but it objected and it won in the end. They ask solicitously after his dick. They hope he will not be incapacitated and that his girlfriend or wife will not be short-changed.

He will never approach a 'lily' in that blithe confident air of youth again. He will approach it with caution, as though it was an enemy with a loaded gun. The army would have taught him one good lesson at least. And he will be careful for the rest of his life when unzipping for a leak.

All of this being said, I must add a rider about gender. Whatever men suffer in this department, women suffer ten times worse. Think of a woman's need for 360-degree privacy, think of the awkwardness of riding breeches and long boots, think of the athleticism needed to balance in a crouch, think of the complications that wind brings to the party, or rain for that matter. My heart goes out to women. My respect too.

Peeing, it would seem is no respecter of gender or age. The humiliations of youth only match those of age. And Ashdown Forest holds its own challenges for any walker or horseman that needs a pee, but thank God, there are, as yet, no 'lilies'.

THE CHURCH IN THE WOOD

A few days ago, my Forest church was 'consecrated', if one may borrow that term from the Catholics and the Church of England.

Zoe and her 14-year-old daughter Courtney went on an exploratory ride to see if they could find their way to the family of giant beech trees which stand cathedral-like in Five Hundred Acre Wood, in close and silent communion with each other.

Zoe is the first to admit that her navigational skills leave a lot to be desired. So she was delighted when, after I heard her out repeating my directions a few times, she managed to find the place. And she had come prepared, as Courtney had asked for a picnic.

So as they sat on their horses, Finch and Mickey, under the winter-bare beeches, they sipped port from a hipflask and ate chocolate brioche. I felt that in doing so they had consecrated my church. The spirit that took them there, a love of the Forest and its quasi-religious qualities, lent their actions more significance than a picnic. Am I being a foolish? Maybe, but indulge me.

People leave Forest offerings around here to commemorate the birthdays of lost loved ones. Because the departed person loved the Forest, the wife, husband or children bring gifts and cards and sometimes balloons tied to a tree or a bench with a favourite view. There is something deeply human in this and something religious too, albeit from an earlier time.

This secret, unspoken religion of the Forest is part ancestor worship, part pagan veneration of a landscape, part tree worship. I understand it well.

The reason I call my 'church' by that name is in part because those lofty beeches really do lend a sense of the sacred to the place. It is always hushed and silent there. And one of the trees bears a 'double font', made of two great cream-coloured fungi growing out of the tree's trunk, one above the other. It does not take much imagination to see this as a place of pilgrimage. And I, for one, never pass through this dell without stopping for a moment's contemplation and prayer.

These days, my prayers are a mix of apologies and thanksgiving. I pray for forgiveness from all those many people I have hurt or let down, knowingly or unknowingly, out of selfishness and ignorance and sometimes fear. My parents, my wife, my siblings, my children, my friends.

And I say thanks for the innumerable blessings in my life. For family, both alive and dead, for old friends and surprising new friends. And for the knowledge that has kept me alive – that it's all about survival. At times, just for the next five minutes if that is all I can manage, and for longer if I can do that. It's about hanging in there.

I pray for kindness, that I be given the grace and patience and wisdom to be kind, as so very many have been kind to me.

And finally, I ask Mother Earth to forgive us the rape and pillage we have made of our time here. A stupidity so monstrous it mocks our arrogance. It may well mean the end of us.

What happened to the Green Man myth, the belief by generations past of a spirit of the forest, the source of all things green and fecund? He is history; his role as the keeper of all plants forgotten. Maybe the time has come to seek him within us and start to worship him again. Perhaps that is the way out of the dead-end in which we've placed ourselves, with just climate activist Greta Thunberg and others like her, bless them, fighting the good fight.

It interests me greatly that the slightly 'woo-woo' business of 'forest bathing' has become so popular, imported from Japan, where Zen has its home. This nature baptism or human communion with the trees is really as old as mankind. After all, we came out of the trees as apes and learned to return to them once we could walk on two legs, as they were a safe place from predators, better than the ground anyway.

Just behind my home, there is a forest plantation which has been sold off in part to a company that offers acre-size plots to people who wish to own a piece of the wood. Here, the small group of new arrivals have erected tents and yurts in a pine wood and they come down from their permanent homes for a spot of woodcraft and forest bathing. I imagine that if you live in a London flat it must almost blow your mind to wake up in your yurt in an East Sussex wood with a stream just below you and the birds in full throat. The mental benefits must be incalculable.

The old Druids are surely smiling. Computers, the internet, artificial intelligence, space travel – and forest bathing. The more things change, the more they stay the same, as the French like to say.

When I plan a ride in the woods, my state of being changes. There is a quickening of energy and interest and anticipation. And as Callum and I slip beneath the Forest canopy, it is as if we have entered a different realm. And, of course, we have. We have left civilisation behind. I am wearing a technologically advanced jacket and carrying a mobile phone, and the hum of traffic is just below the level of hearing. So, like a space-walking astronaut, I am still attached by an umbilical cord to safety. But out in space, as in the woods, things are not civilised, and stuff happens out there. This sharpens all your senses and connects you to the unseen. As a result, you feel more alive: you are more of an animal than you were half an hour ago, sitting on the couch at home.

People out walking or riding on the Forest seldom look glum. They are enjoying themselves and their faces show it. But there are others who make their way here to end their lives. Their idea is to be among beloved woodland, their last sight of the earth before death claims them, rather than to be staring at a wall. I can understand that. It is an act of will, choosing your time and your place to bid the world farewell. How many people, dying of Covid-19 in a hospital, surrounded by medical paraphernalia, by other patients and by the hospital staff, yearned for one last look at nature before they closed their eyes? Ashdown is a place of celebration, and it is also a place of earthly departure and a last resting place. The ashes of many lie here, caressed by the wind and kissed by the rain.

To think of the Forest as a kind of church is not that unusual, I think. There are places here where people leave offerings, jewellery, crucifixes and of course pots of honey for Pooh Bear. All these objects are manmade, but they are left to link the giver with who knows what? But we do know that they feel close to something greater than themselves, this thing that they find by being in the woods.

How strange that William Cobbett in his *Sussex Journal* entry of 8 January 1822 described Ashdown Forest as a bleak wasteland. He wrote:

> 'At about three miles from Grinstead you come to a pretty village, called Forest-Row, and then, on the road to Uckfield, you cross Ashurst (*sic*) Forest, which is a heath, with here and there a few birch scrubs upon it, verily the most villainously ugly spot I saw in England. This lasts you for five miles, getting, if possible, uglier and uglier all the way, till, at last, as if barren soil, nasty spewy gravel, heath and even that stunted, were not enough, you see some rising spots, which instead of trees, present you with black, ragged, hideous rocks.'

He must have been having a bad day. Or maybe he was picking up on the local vibe, which is not particularly civilised.

Sussex, it must be admitted, has a pagan past. It was the last Saxon county to be converted to Christianity. No one even tried until St Wilfrid in the 680s, and the new religion remained unpopular in the county for centuries to come.

William the Conqueror was still issuing laws to stamp out paganism hereabouts in his day. The area's wild unruly reputation persisted until at least the sixteenth century. Criminals, highwaymen and a league of baddies used the Forests that covered the Weald as a hideout before the Tudor and Stuart kings unleashed a programme of tree felling to smelt iron and build ships.

And even today beneath the area's polite veneer, the old gods still walk the woods, I have no doubt. And my so-called church would make a perfect place for some after-dark revelry.

As Callum and I once more enter this intimate tree-columned space, I think how few churches would welcome a horseman clip clopping up the nave to the font. In the far distance, I can hear a dog bark and the shrill voices of excited children. The horse, I realise, has been listening to this too for some minutes, well before the sound reached my ears. But these visitors take another path, and the sounds fade. Now it is just the faintest breath of wind high above me in the branched rafters and above that only sky. The Forest stands mute once more, holding a horseman and his horse by a power that neither understands but which draws them back, again and again to this place, this magical place, this place of worship.

Julian Roup

WOMEN AND HORSES

Growing up in South Africa's Cape in the 1950s and 1960s, I was out on a limb – neither a rugby player nor a surfer. That left me with a distinct disadvantage when it came to girls. My passions were reading and horse riding. Thank God for horses! They were my wingmen in the dating game.

When the good Lord got round to designing women and horses he must have been in the best of moods, because he used everything at his disposal to create two of the most beautiful creatures on earth. When I first observed the combination of the two – girls riding horses – it was love at first sight.

And despite the fact that I was hopeless at maths, I soon realised that at any riding stables, I was outnumbered by a factor of around twenty to one by girls. How it is that so few boys ever woke up to this fact is beyond me. On the beaches of the Cape, where admittedly, there were beautiful girls aplenty, there were just as many boys. The rugby field was even less hopeful. The field was packed with thirty rugged types with ten times as many watching from the side-lines, including a thin sprinkling of girls. And surfing was utterly hopeless. There were literally hundreds of god-like Adonises for the handful of hardy girls on the beach. The stables, on the other hand, were awash with girls and lovely women, and just a handful of boys and men.

I soon found that even those girls who did not ride generally appreciated horses. So the scene was set for a teenage Bacchanal. Sadly, that never happened. I was tall, skinny, bespectacled and shy. Painfully shy. A bookworm. Not the stuff of teenage dreams.

But the South African sun tanned me, the riding muscled me up into better shape, I got prescription sunglasses, and my riding improved. I started early in the mornings and got home mid-afternoon. I became something of a distance rider, a cowboy. Almost always riding alone.

During the summer, my family moved to our holiday home on the coast at Bloubergstrand, which has breath-taking views of Table Mountain across the bay. There was wonderful beach riding to be had and vast inland sand dunes, plus miles and miles of uninhabited Port Jackson scrub country to explore. Each summer, I moved my horse to Ivy Marsicano's Santiago stables, about five miles away from our home by the sea.

The stables were built to look like a Western ranch and attracted filmmakers now and then. Each summer a troupe of Spanish dancers and musicians, touring the country, would come out for a day's riding, and in the evening, Ivy would organize a barbecue. As dusk fell and the day cooled, the Spanish guitars would start their lament and on an impromptu stage, made of packing cases and plywood, the tap-dancing shoes would begin to drum.

The combination of a day's riding in sunshine, youthful high spirits, beer and that insistent, commanding music that demanded a response, was intoxicating. The women and men in their Spanish costumes dancing in the firelight, the drama of the dance, sensual and harsh in equal measure, spoke of a deep human need as old as man. The show would last an hour at most, but its effect stayed with me all my life, with a love of Spanish guitar and of Spanish dancing.

Years later, driving across the north Spanish plain near the city of Salamanca, the car radio offered up Rodrigo's *Concierto de Aranjuez* with electrifying effect. The vast barren plain at dusk, the music and my memories took me back to Santiago and all that it had meant.

When I was 16, I asked a girl, a friend of my sister, to come riding with me and she accepted. I packed a picnic and a blanket in my saddlebags and together we rode down past Zeekoeivlei to the beach at Strandfontein on the False Bay coast. On the way back, we stopped at the lake and had our picnic. I don't know what I had expected, but it was all perfectly innocent except for an electric charge between us which I felt and I know she felt too – years later she told me so. But we ate the sandwiches and fruit I had packed and drank the Cokes and then, after a while, rode back to the stables. I can remember my frustration.

In time this passed, and not surprisingly over the years, I had a number of girlfriends who rode. And I learned that going riding on a first date for four hours or more was not advisable. Many of the poor girls could barely stand afterwards. So horses and riding were left to later in the relationship. That worked admirably for everyone.

The Cape offers magnificent riding country – the beaches, the Forests, the mountains. And in summer, the nights are warm. I remember one night riding in moonlight with a girl who frankly rode better than me. We made our way slowly up the coast from Bloubergstrand towards Melkbosstrand at low tide, with more than a 100-yard width of hard flat sand to canter on. There was bioluminescence in the water, so that as the horses walked knee-deep in the sea, they left a trail of light beneath and behind them. It was unforgettable, echoed as it was by the moonlight and the Milky Way.

There is something special in the relationship women have with horses. They seduce each other. I'm not sure who leads the seduction, the girl or the horse. Safe to say it is a partnership that is magic to observe.

Years later in Sussex I rode with Jan up on the South Downs, both during warm summer days and bright moonlight nights, the moonlight reflecting off the white chalk paths that criss-cross the miles of whale-backed Downs. As we rode in an enchanted silence, the lights of ships in the Channel passed to one side of us and the lights of the villages below twinkled all the way to the North Downs.

A woman riding takes on all the strength, mystery and grace of the horse and reflects her own mystery, strength and grace back to the animal. They are no longer two beings but one, a very powerful new thing. A man on a horse projects force. A woman on a horse is something more than that. You only have to watch the world-beating dressage rider, Charlotte Dujardin, riding Valegro at the very highest point of this challenging discipline, to know that what you are watching is sublime, two great artists making beauty tangible.

Or simpler yet, a girl cantering a horse on a beach, manes of hair flying. What can touch that for grace? And to touch one deeply, the image of Jan's horses who have all followed her like dogs, not needing lead ropes.

The bond between women and their horses has to be seen to be believed. Just this week, Jan was out riding Traveller on Ashdown Forest when he tripped in some boggy mud and fell down on his side, throwing her clear. Muddied but unhurt and unbowed, she remounted her mud-covered horse and the two rode home quite happily. That is trust. The next day to the amazement of her stable friends, she and Traveller were once again out on the Forest on her birthday. The woman-horse deal is not broken by a fall.

Often the first thing she will do on getting back from a ride is to write down the poems that have come to her while out riding. Like rain or sun, they have fallen on her skin or dazzled her eyes, and the words stay with her through the miles of Forest trails, so that when they appear on paper, it is as though they have come from the trees; poems as fruit.

In her powerful and remarkable book *Pip Pip*, author Jay Griffiths writes about wilderness. My belief is that wilderness is also something women tap into when they are on horseback. However domesticated we think horses are, that is to misunderstand their nature as prey animals. They will bolt, buck, rear, bite and kick to escape anything that frightens them; that wild instinct to survive lives deep within them and that is what you are on when you venture out into the Forest on horseback.

Griffiths writes:

'Wilderness is a ferocious intoxication which sweeps over your senses with rinsing vitality, leaving stripped to the vivid, your senses rubbed until they shine. It is an untouched place which touches you deeply, and its aftermath – when landscape becomes innerscape – leaves you elated, awed and changed utterly. Forget the lullaby balm of nature tame as a well-fed lawn, here nature has a lean and violent waking grandeur which will not let you sleep… It is an aphrodisiac; it is a place of furious fecundity – not virginal, but erupting with the unenclosable passion at the volcanic heart of life.'

Kapow! She knows what she is talking about. Women on horseback are shapeshifting into another form, allowing them access to wilderness, leaving manners and civility and civilisation as far behind as a dying planet. No wonder they love horses.

Julian Roup

THREE LOCKDOWNS ON ASHDOWN – A WORD MAP

This place has been home for almost 40 years, and in this last plague year of March 2020 to January 2021 it has held Jan and me safe during three lockdowns, the third now a week old, with at least another six weeks to go. Is it any wonder that I feel a powerful connection to this land of heath and forest so far from the land of my birth and my first 30 years on earth, the Cape in South Africa?

I know this country like few know it thanks to four decades of walking and riding it. I know its streams, its woods, its wide open spaces, its hills and its valleys. I know how to escape the worst of its weather by sheltering in the lee of its contours, keeping to valley bottoms, and on bright warm spring and summer days, Callum and I make our patrols on the high ground that offers commanding views to the South Downs, the North Downs, west to Gatwick and east to Crowborough and beyond.

I know the places the deer know, the home of the fox and the badger, the antheaps, the leaping squirrel and the sliding adders. I watch the sky with its crows and wood pigeons, its buzzards and owls, its bats, the robins and the wrens, the blackbirds and the Forest's opera singers, the skylarks. And in spring I wait for and celebrate the arrival of my fellow African travellers, the swallows. They bring me news each year that my homeland still exists and offers them succour. Their presence overhead in our garden and their nests in our stables are a blessing. They are my most welcome guests and the ones I miss the most on their departure.

As I live here so intensely, is it any surprise that I have looked beyond my life to where I would like my remains to be scattered, to know that the landscape that has so filled my heart and soul will have my bones, as ash, to enrich its soil? A son of the African Southland, now forever part of the European North, I am enmeshed in the yo-yo of my ancestors, from Africa to Europe, millennia ago and more recently from

Europe to Africa and then, for me, one last trek back to Europe, to live my life beneath pale skies and soft light.

I know this place as intimately as my hands and its soil lies beneath my fingernails quite regularly. I breathe its tree-breath and its gorse breath and its bracken-breath and inhale deep of its fungus and pine smells and with wonder I wander beneath its luminous spring light under the neon green of new leaf. This place has entered me; its DNA is now part of my own.

Lockdown is a term mediated by the freedom to roam we have here. I do not live hemmed in by four walls, even though plague stalks the land. How could my love for this place, already deep, not be deepened these past 12 months as I move, alive still, through its wooded corridors and open pastures, its secret spaces and its public walks? After all, it is home.

January 2021 sees me more constrained than usual by the rapidly spreading new strain of the Covid-19 virus. We are in a race with this plague which is making fearful inroads. Some 1,300 people died yesterday, and the vaccine is still a month off arriving locally. It is a race for life. I am hunkered down in the cottage, having given up caring for and riding my horse Callum. Three women have tested positive at the stable yard next door, and my friend Zoe has taken on the responsibility for Callum. I am grateful to know he is in such caring hands.

I receive a sixth letter from the Department of Health and Social Care which both concerns me and also fills me with a warm feeling that for once I am being monitored for my wellbeing. For once, the Government does not want anything more from me but my continued life. How novel.

> 'As part of the lockdown, the Government is also advising all clinically extremely vulnerable people to take extra shielding measures to protect themselves. This advice will apply until 21 February 2021. If the advice is to continue beyond that date, we will write to you again with further information.

104

'We are writing to you because you have previously been identified as someone thought to be clinically extremely vulnerable and therefore at highest risk of becoming very unwell if you catch COVID-19. This letter contains important advice on how to protect yourself and how to access further support.'

With this advice ringing in my ears, I tell Zoe, Callum's new carer, that if she and her mother Kim are caught on horseback, trespassing, by the land agent in the De La Warr part of Hundred Acre Wood she should say that the old boy has died and she is taking his horse on a farewell pilgrimage – a fine story that might get her off the hook. And, if I do survive, the story offers the hope that when I am next seen trespassing, the land agent will get the horrors and give me a wide berth, thinking he is seeing a ghost. A sort of win-win situation. The trick of it requires me to live.

Jan and I now exercise up our lane, passing others doing the same. And then we scurry home and close the front door tight. My journeys across the Forest now take place in my head. It is a 'stations of the cross' kind of meandering, touching base with the central focus of each Forest valley. Crossing the few roads is safer this way; I only have my disembodied self to carry across, no horse to worry about being frightened by some loud truck or motorbike. The dogs no longer bother me either, as I ghost past.

There is good news abroad. Trump is almost part of history, and Joe Biden and Kamala Harris wait in the wings, just ten days to their inauguration.

The storming of the Capitol was a dark new stain on Trump's much besmirched soul. But his presidency has been functional. If America will only listen, it has shown how close democracy has come to the edge, thanks to the chasm between rich and poor, fertile ground for revolution. Trump may well have served as an inoculation against fascism if the lessons of his Presidency are learned. If not, the next would-be dictator may just end America's existence as a beacon of freedom, the virus in the White House worse in the long run than the pandemic.

And here in the UK, despite incompetence and corruption, and Boris' pitiful pretence at leadership, a vaccine has been developed that could be our saving grace. The trick now is not to die on the last day of the war, but to hang in until the cavalry arrives in a hypodermic needle.

As I wait, I make mental pilgrimages to my favourite destinations on the Forest. Ashdown is divided up by a number of roads. The A22, the A275, the B2026, the B1288 and the charming small country lane at the far southern outskirt of the Forest called Cackle Street which runs between the A22 south of Nutley to the B2026 Duddleswell Road, a lane where a modest equestrian property will set you back £1m and more. The road east-west across the Forest from Poundgate to Nutley with its cattle grids that hold the sheep and cattle in this area and which also features three car parks near Ellison's Ponds and Friends Clump. These are the motor arteries of the Forest which bring car-borne walkers in from local villages and towns as well as places further afield. I am not the only pilgrim on these roads. In fact, I have never seen the car parks so rammed as during these lockdowns. The Forest, our country lung, is giving those thousands cooped up at home some respite, some air and exercise, for them and their animals.

The foxy estate agents are licking their chops as well-heeled Londoners stream out of the city now in search of rural escapes. The attractions of the city have nosedived thanks to the threat posed by the density of the population. When the threat is other people, it's best to be where these carriers are thinnest on the ground. Residents of SW1 and all parts nearby are off to the country if they don't already own a country bolthole.

There are, as I count them, nine distinct areas of Ashdown Forest, all with destinations worth a visit by foot or on horseback.

My home turf, the bit of the Forest closest to me, holds Five Hundred Acre Wood and runs from Church Hill car park on the B2881 south just short of Kings Standing and then does a U-turn to run alongside the Hartfield Road the B2026 to just below the Enchanted Place to the west. And just behind the cottage is the area of Ashdown below the orthopaedic hospital, the Horder Centre, which once had Princess Margaret as its President. They still speak kindly of her there, maybe the last place in the UK to do so, other than in the home of Colin Tennant's widow Anne, Baroness Glenconner, who introduced the Princess and her then husband, Anthony Armstrong Jones, to their Caribbean hideaway, Mustique. We are not short of glamour in these parts. William the Conqueror strode this way, as did King Harold just before he received a Norman arrow in the eye at Hastings. Henry VIII hunted here too. And then of course there was President John F. Kennedy, American royalty, visiting Prime Minister, Harold MacMillan, and going to church in Forest Row.

Directly due south of our cottage is the circuit of the Forest that takes in King's Standing Clump, looping east down to the Crow & Gate Pub and up the hill south west to the radio masts. Great views to the South Downs beyond Lewes lie before you from the pine clump on the southerly end. Here there are two great uphill grassy gallops. In the King's Standing car park is a year-round ice cream van, if you feel in need of sustenance.

The 'Big Bowl' as we call it, just across the road from the radio masts, holds pleasures aplenty. At its heart is Old Lodge, the estate owned by a Saudi Arabian Prince, His Highness Prince Torki Bin Mohammed Bin Saud Al Kabeer. The house was built by Henry VIII in the sixteenth century and has always been used as a hunting lodge, but now it is a stud breeding show-jumpers.

Prince Torki must be the only Saudi show jumping horse breeder whose homebred horse has won a medal at the Olympic Games. As the breeder of Sultan V, a team bronze medallist at the London Olympics in 2012, he gained respect worldwide.

Old Lodge, the 180-acre stud which the Prince bought twenty years ago, boasts a unique location. The main house, which looks south to Friend's Clump, is a huge manor with massive walls, impressive decoration, and wonderful views.

Pictures in the house show the Prince in meetings with George W. Bush, Nelson Mandela, the presidents of China, Argentina, and many other heads of state.

The view of Old Lodge looking north from Friend's Clump or west from Camp Hill Clump is one of the finest on the Forest. I sometimes wonder if the Prince ever uses binoculars to monitor riders galloping up these hills adjacent to his property?

Below Old Lodge runs a small stream with a little waterfall, known as 'The Garden of Eden' and there is something pristine about it. But even the most irreligious among us would not wish the winter temperatures around here on poor Adam and Eve, living in the buff.

The bridge crossing the stream here is always busy with walkers, dogs and children. Over the years, I've had the odd bit of excitement with various horses dancing across that bridge, keeping an eye out for the dogs and kids playing in the streambed just above and below the bridge. And it was near here that Jan ran into some trouble with a bull terrier off its lead which kept jumping up at Sebastian, our bay gelding, trying to get a grip on his nose. She was surrounded by a huge crowd of people and children on a sponsored dog walk ... that was where part of the danger lay. If she'd fallen off, he would have galloped through them.

The horse finally reared and lashed out at the barking animal with his hooves, breaking one of the dog's legs. The dog owner was understandably upset, but probably had no idea of what might have happened to Jan and Sebastian if the dog had got its teeth into the horse's nose. All three might have died in the carnage that would have followed. Sometimes dog walkers and horse riders are not the best of friends.

Adjacent to Old Lodge, there are hundreds of acres of army land used for manoeuvres and you hear the odd rumble of explosives now and then. The Big Bowl also holds Ellison's Ponds and the remains of an old Roman Road on the ridge running up to Camp Hill Clump. Here our footprints intersect with those of the Roman legions who passed this way when England was an outpost of the Roman Empire. This grassy valley holds more than just grazing sheep and cattle. The ghosts of Tudor Kings and Roman Emperors stand looking across at Prince Torki's stud, assessing the youngstock.

To the south, beyond the Big Bowl, lies the southerly slope that holds the Airman's Grave. This area has four walking and riding loops, three to the west and one on the other side of the Duddleswell Road. This is one of the sunniest and best-drained parts of the Forest and the views down to Lewes and the South Downs are lovely. It's great galloping country if you have a sure-footed horse, for here, as everywhere on the Forest, there are ridges and ruts and boggy bits. The best place for fast work on horseback is to the east of the road near the village of Fairwarp, which after a steep dip, provides a lovely long, grassy canter track.

Just above Cackle Street is an area of enchanting river crossings, which in winter is very wet, but is lovely in summer. It's a good place to teach a young horse to deal with ditches, streams and bridges, well out of the public eye.

Due west of Friend's Clump, you enter another Forest landscape, the one abutting the Nutley Windmill and on the other side of the valley, Millbrook, and the A22 Nutley to Forest Row road. This is where Traveller lives at a small yard, as the place guarantees the year-round turnout that suits his need to keep moving. Although we kept our horses together for almost three decades, in many ways it makes sense for two writers to ride alone, letting the voices of the Forest and our various influences make themselves heard. It is a process that has served us well, as the ten books the old cottage has produced will attest.

The estate that is home to the yard runs festivals and other events, including cycle races and fancy dress fun runs. It is also a base to the Army. So the horses here have to get used to explosions, mock battles and festival paraphernalia from bouncy castles, bunting, over-excited children wanting a ride, and people pulling heavy-wheeled cases across the grass, to all the smells of a small encampment with exotic cooking scents mixed in. Traveller takes it all in his stride.

Across the A22 is a further area of Forest, home to a Second World War emergency aircraft landing strip. This may be where the young airmen had hoped to land but they got it wrong if so; too far south-east by about a mile. Today the landing strip offers great space to canter on clay. This area leads to Birch Grove and the Red Lion pub and through the woods to Chelwood Gate and down a lane to the lovely foodie haven, the Coach & Horses pub.

North of the 'Big Bowl' is the area of the Forest that includes the Enchanted Place, the Hollow on the Hill and on down the hill to Pooh Sticks Bridge at one side and The Hatch Inn at the other, a good place to pull up a horse for a break and for a rider to get a pint of beer. Now you are firmly in the storied world of A.A. Milne. Here lives Eeyore, Tigger, Piglet and Owl, and their friend Christopher Robin, who was so horrified by his celebrity childhood that he did a runner to Devon to sell books and never came back.

And finally, west of The Hatch lies the Ridge Road, home to the Ashdown Forest Centre and along from it, views overlooking the Royal Ashdown Forest Golf Club. There is riding on either side of this road, the one area pure heath, the other woodland. This is where the poets Ezra Pound and W.B. Yeats walked and wrote for three winters from 1913 to 1916, based at Stone Cottage near The Hatch.

In these Forest 'rooms' I have lived my life for four decades. It is a small world, just ten miles square, and sometimes I ask myself how someone who criss-crossed Africa, Europe and America was able to settle for such a small piece of land to call home? The answer, I suppose, is its beauty, its literary links, its welcome to horse riders, its views and its decidedly spooky magic. I have found it more than enough. Truly, sometimes less is indeed more. And when you are ordered by the government to stay home in lockdown, the miles of Ashdown are a veritable feast to exercise in, to think and to dream.

If ever you pass a grey-bearded man on a magnificent chestnut that looks more horse than he can handle, and you hear him singing lullabies to the horse in a strange language, you will have walked past me, or my ghost, depending on the outcome of the third lockdown.

ALL CHANGE

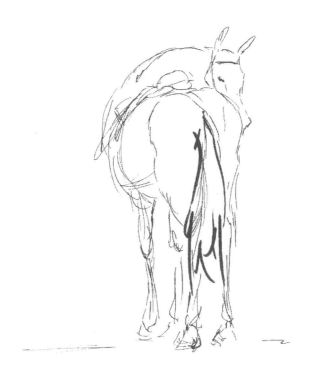

Julian Roup

R iding locally is not all fun, games and Forest bathing. There are things afoot that sadden me, even though I know that change is inevitable. For 40 years I have been privileged to ride the miles of Ashdown Forest and its adjacent wooded areas, undisturbed by change, but now that happy state of affairs is ending. It is being threatened by a number of things.

The most obvious recent impact is the huge surge in the number of walkers desperate for an escape from Covid-19 incarceration, and who can blame them? But the vastly increased numbers of people and dogs on the Forest does detract from what we all so love about it, the peace and quiet it offers us. But in time, as the vaccination programme takes hold, hopefully things will return to normal.

This I fear is not so for some of the adjacent areas. The forestry land which lies behind our cottage is undergoing something of a revolution. A part of it has been sold off and is being used as a sort of adventure playground for young people, which involves a shooting range and regular explosions. How this ever came to pass in an Area of Outstanding Natural Beauty is beyond me, and my heart goes out to those living in neighbouring properties. When riding past it on the trail alongside the road I am tense, hoping Callum and I will be well past before any explosions take place. There are warning signs and a recorded warning message broadcasting to passers-by the need to be alert to the possibility of noise from the firing range. Once, there was just the sound of the birds and the hum of the odd passing car.

I am not sure how Callum would react to the sound of a grenade going off nearby. But what really concerns me is what might happen if a child on a pony rode by just as an explosion took place. With cars passing just ten foot away, the potential for disaster is huge. Many of us have written to our local authority and our MP about this but as yet have had no constructive information about how this state of affairs came about, or how it might be made safe, or best of all, ended.

Elsewhere in the woodland are people pitching tents or building yurts to enjoy a woodland experience. Recently I saw that one of these campers had made a large fire outside his tent in the middle of a pine forest. The potential for a wildfire to take hold was so obvious I could only wonder at this stupidity and think of the animals that would die in such an event.

I am only too aware that my views are selfish. Why should others not also enjoy the Forest in their own way? The difference is that my impacts are only hoofmarks and a greeting as I pass by.

The threats to the sanctity of this place come from the air as well. For some years now, the traffic in and out of Gatwick has increased. This plague year has brought one huge benefit: an end to overhead aircraft noise, which has all but ceased but for 20 flights a week compared to the 50 an hour in normal times. But the threat of a second runway at Gatwick is not entirely resolved, and if it went ahead would mean ever-greater aerial disturbance. It is not only the noise that is the problem. Aircraft overhead leave a trail of engine fuel fumes which settle on the land below, a toxic poison which infiltrates the plants, animals and doubtless humans too.

Some change is good. Callum has become a much more chilled horse after 18 months of hacking on the Forest. He no longer, or very seldom, does his triple-lutz move, whirling away again and again from something scary. If something alarms him now he may start, but a word from me will usually get him moving forward again and I give him a pat of encouragement. He knows me and I think trusts me to take care of him. He knows his new turf now too, well enough to 'suggest' a faster way home, by trying to turn down a path he knows.

One new change in him amuses me greatly. Like our other horse, Traveller, he has become something of a 'people person'. When walkers approach, I feel him slowing down, ready for a chat. He has come to expect this, as quite often these days people will greet me and comment on Callum and I will stop for a chat. The horse is always only too happy to stand and be admired. He seems happy in his gleaming copper gold skin.

I wish I could say the same for his rider. My years of riding have taken a toll and I am more creaky than I would like to be, but it is a price I do not regret. The pleasure that riding has given me, the books it has given me, the friends it has given me, the wife it has given me, the country I have crossed, are gifts that I would not be without. The creakiness seems a small price to pay. There are other, more ominous changes, but medical science seems to be holding these at bay for now. The Sword of Damocles hanging over me does one profoundly important thing; it makes me value and appreciate each day and each ride so much more than in the past. It has sharpened my powers of observation too. I notice more and I value it more.

I embrace the changes wrought by the natural turning of the year more than ever. It is as if I have more educated ears, better vision and a sharper sense of smell. The opposite in fact is true. But the focus they bring now makes me appreciate what they note that much more. In a way my infirmities bring a blessing – a vision of the world that is sharper and more beautiful. I glory in the spring, bathe in the summer, am embraced by autumn and warmed by winter. I live more fully it seems, even as my vitality wanes. There is a last bonfire of my strength, more smoke than flame. Change is coming and I must accept it with as much grace as I can muster.

Change on the Forest comes too in the increasing numbers of deer killed on Forest roads. The annual slaughter of the deer population by motorists runs to hundreds of these iconic animals that die terrible deaths. We have as yet not found a solution to this problem. That is a change I would welcome.

This is not a pristine paradise. How could it be, being so close to one of the great cities of the planet? It is a miracle that it exists at all. But for how much longer?

Over the years, I have sat astride many horses looking out over this landscape in dreamy reverie. Now and then, in summer, on a windless evening, I will see a hot air balloon drifting north, as will the horse, in due course. Some horses stand steadfast, some dance around as the whoosh! of the balloon burners adds lift, and I wave to the passengers in the basket hung below it. The moment always holds something magical about it and I envy them their height and the vantage it gives them to look out across the whole of my small kingdom.

There is one place that commands a view of a private hidden valley farm that I like to ride to and just stand and stare. Its fields often hold a herd of deer, grazing close to the woods in case of danger. The sky above it is worked by a pair of buzzards making their eerie cry, in search of prey. This place has remained the same, the land anyway, but the old farmhouse has given way to a three storied extravaganza of a home with pillars and great arched windows, more in keeping with Belgravia than Ashdown. Other homes in the area have also fallen prey to wealthy new owners whose fantasies are not to my taste.

Despite such changes, I am hopeful that Ashdown will stay enough as it is to see me out, but my children will inherit a diminished Forest I fear, less wild, less magical, more trammelled.

We need to rise up and be counted, to speak in its defence, or we too, we who love it, will go the way of the deer, mowed down by speeding people who are more interested in their destination than in their journey. We will all be the poorer without it.

A Horseman's Fear

Horses are unpredictable creatures and the gentlest and kindest among them is perfectly capable of killing its rider intentionally or unintentionally. Anyone who throws a leg over a horse's back knows, or should know, or is soon to learn, that some care needs to be taken. The harshness of not learning this lesson could include the loss of your life. I make no apologies for sounding wimpish. As they say in Afrikaans: '*Liewers bang Jan as dooie Jan!*' 'Better scared John than dead John'.

It must be said at the outset that youth brings with it a much more laissez-faire attitude to riding than is available to older riders. But inevitably you reach a certain age when you begin to lose some of the boyish bottle of your teens and twenties. If this fear becomes dominant, then it is time to pack it in and find a comfy sofa that stays in one place. I've not quite reached that point yet, but doubtless that day will arrive.

I've had my moments with horses. My damaged knees caused by my horse Quest when he reared up and fell over backwards onto me, pinning my legs for a moment before he scrambled clear. At some point, replacement knees will be needed. The worst thing about this fall was that it was a self-inflicted wound, not the horse's fault but mine. I was tired after a day in the saddle, heading home through the dune country near False Bay coast in Cape Town and approaching Zeekoeivlei. Quest, keen to get home himself, kept jogging instead of walking. I was hot, tired and getting more and more annoyed with him and I did what no decent horseman should ever do – I gave him a stiff jerk on the reins. He had quite a strong bit in his mouth as he could take a hold at the gallop. Hurt and surprised by my yanking his mouth, he reared up to escape the pain and toppled over backwards onto me.

This scene runs through my mind each and every time

a new anaesthetist says: 'Goodnight, sunshine,' as I am wheeled into the operating theatre once more. A tough lesson, learned the hard way. I have never yanked on a horse's mouth with anything like such force ever again. But it was too late for my crocked knees. Temper on horseback is best jettisoned fast.

But this is an extreme example of what can go wrong while out riding. Not so long ago, riding on our equine saint, Traveller, up behind the Duddleswell tearooms on Ashdown Forest. I was exploring a new path in an attempt to find the stableyard of a friend of ours, when the horse stepped into a hole and went down as if pole-axed. He managed to find his feet and came back up again but the violence of the motion tore something in my groin and I hobbled around for a few weeks after that.

Jan has twice survived unscathed (touch wood) when Traveller has fallen with her on the Forest going over sideways, once on ice and once in mud.

I once had a lovely Irish Sport Horse, a bright chestnut with a white blaze called Max, whom Jan hunter-trialled and showed in a working hunter class, taking the red rosette. He was a sensible sort, but could get lit up out on the Forest on a cold day. Riding just north of Nutley, to the west of the A22 near the car park at the brow of the hill, Max planted himself one day and refused to move on. There was a lovely level piece of bright green grass ahead of us, but he was having none of it. He stood immovable. I thought I knew better and that he was being unreasonable, and I pushed him on. Good horse that he was, he overcame his instincts, stepped into what was a hidden bog and sank right up to his girth. My quaking legs now stood on the quaking grass. It took some doing to get him out of there. Covered in mud, the two of us made our way home, the rider older and wiser and more inclined to listen to his horse in future.

But these are extreme examples of fear-inducing events on horseback. The more usual run-of-the-mill excitements occur when a piece of paper or plastic blows across your path and the horse shies violently. Pheasants can be a menace too, sitting tight in the long grass until you are right above them, when they literally explode into flight. As does the horse you are riding. I've certainly had a few Pegasus experiences in my time, when I've been higher off the ground than I would care to be without a ladder.

Then there are the horses with a sense of humour or a skittish nature. Rearing, bucking, shying, all have their place in the repertoire of horses who feel it's time for a break from their irritating rider, who wants to keep on going instead of going home, as any sensible horse would prefer after a few hours out on the Forest. As these incidents add up, another drop goes out of the boldness bottle and another drop of caution enters.

Now add vast open spaces and a cold biting wind. That is quite often a recipe for excitement, if not disaster. Some for sale adverts will be honest to a fault and admit that the horse in question is not one that enjoys hacking on its own. Fair enough; these are herd animals and they know well enough that being alone means that you are the only target for a predator, as there are no other horsey friends or relatives to choose from. It's probably the more intelligent kind of horse that will not take kindly to wandering lonely as a cloud on the Forest.

Now add wind. Wind and horses don't generally go together. Wind sets horses off. It makes them skittish and silly, and liable to get into a pickle. I don't know why this is, but it is something you can generally rely on.

The list of things to fear when you are riding include ruts, ice, bog, mud, rivers, bridges, pheasants, paper, plastic, cars, trucks and motorbikes, low hanging branches, puddles of water, deer, cattle, sheep, kites, drones, helicopters, dogs and walkers in bizarre gear who hide in the bushes, trying not to frighten the horse. I could go on and on – the list of what would spook a horse is endless. And there are new things added each day.

Let's take a day in point. It is a cold grey one with a bitter wind blowing. The horse has been stable-bound for a few days as it's been tipping down with rain and you haven't fancied getting wet. There has been no turnout so the horse must be exercised, as each day in the box will make him ever more pent-up. Your gut feels tight with tension as you saddle up. If you are sensible, you will lunge the horse for 20 minutes, trotting him on the end of a rope in the sand school, working the worst of the crazies off him. But sometimes you either don't have the time or the inclination and you pile on, figuring that there are enough hills to knock some of the nonsense out of him before you are out on the open top of the Forest. This plan works well, and the puffed horse is soon topside and behaving nicely. Half an hour in, he has got his second wind, and the wind blowing across the Forest is playing with his tail and mane. Far across on the other valley slope is a rider cantering a horse up a hill. All hell breaks loose. Barnum and Bailey Circus would snap your horse up for his airs above the ground. A Western rodeo might have good use for him.

If you are lucky, you manage to control him, cursing the other rider. If unlucky, he goes home without you and you and your wounded dignity (or broken arm) walk home dejected, hoping that a car does not knock the idiot horse over when he crosses the two roads between him and home.

But forget about wind. You knew what you were getting into. Let's take a perfect, warm summer's day, no wind, just peace settling slow on the Forest. You've been out riding for two hours and the horse is well exercised. You are riding home 'on the buckle' as they say, with your reins loose, all is right with the world and you are looking forward to a cold beer and supper.

As you cross the last road before home, a cyclist comes out of nowhere, silently but at speed, and suddenly the horse is running for his life as you grab for the yards of flapping rein. The horse is bolting downhill over ruts and loose shale, as if the hounds of hell were after him. That is all that it takes to set him off.

An industry in safety gear has been set up to protect both horse and rider from mishap. For the rider there is now the equivalent of the exploding safety airbag in a car. This piece of gear is a vest you wear with a string attached to your saddle. If you and the saddle part company, a cylinder of compressed air will inflate the vest into a fat cushion all round your chest, neck and back before you hit the deck. There are various kinds of back protectors, technologically advanced helmets and many other things to help you stay safe. They all have their place. That said, other than a helmet I have as yet not taken to air vests or anything else. My bad, perhaps.

If you ride on the Forest these days, you are required to have £5m in Third Party insurance just in case the un-guided missile you are riding decides to take it into its head to run down an unsuspecting walker or crash into a car. You need a good imagination to even start the list of what horses are capable of once they are set on wreaking havoc.

Is it any wonder that the older rider takes his courage and sticks it tight to the sticking place before mounting a horse? It is best to have your eyes open wide and your senses on full alert when setting out for the Forest. Or you could indeed be in for a big surprise.

As I get into my riding boots and put on my sweat-soiled leather chaps, my crash helmet and my jacket with a pocket up front in easy reach for my mobile phone, I some-times wonder why I am still riding at seventy? To understand why, you will have to get on a horse yourself, and if you ride you will need no explanation. There is nothing else like it. Nothing exists like it to connect you to the deep past and the near past, to activate your primordial animal instincts, to make you feel so utterly alive and in love with life. Fear is a small price to pay.

GRAB A BITE

Julian Roup

One of the joys of riding is the way it keeps the weight off you. You can pretty much eat what you like. The mucking out, grooming, exercising, walking the horse to and from his field, all add to calories burned. And it's fair to say that riding sharpens the appetite. These for me are the bolt-on blessings of being a horseman – appetite at no cost to the waist.

I know soon enough if I need to do more exercise or eat less as Callum has a vocal way of encouraging this by grunting meaningfully when I get on his back. An equine equivalent of 'Ooomph!'

Around the Forest we are blessed with some of the best farm shops in the area. Lockdown has unearthed an abundance of small independent food suppliers who deliver to your door. I've had some of the best meat and vegetable produce I've tasted, pork chops, steak, sausages, pies, bread, vegetables and fruit.

For a meat eater with a conscience, it's good to have the Forest Row producer Tablehurst Farm Shop on our doorstep. Tablehurst is a biodynamic farm that produces everything on the premises from scratch, ready for the shop to sell.

Cherry Gardens Farm Shop is another of our local discoveries. This charming farm shop, surrounded in summer by a haze of flowers, has 33 acres under cultivation, with six huge polytunnels and propagation tunnels where they raise everything from seed. All their fruit and veg is grown to certified organic standards. It is always a pleasure to shop here as one gets to know the team who run it and they get to know you.

The place is also worth a visit to pick your own fruit and veg in season or to choose from the acres of flowers they produce. There are shady benches for picnics too. The place is something of an oasis. That said, neither of these two local producers is cheap, but then you get what you pay for: Superb produce, which for a bread lover includes a great selection of sourdough and other breads and rolls.

Another local gem is Plaw Hatch Farm Shop just outside Sharpethorne. Here you will find a full range of produce such as milk, cheese and yoghurt, meat, fruit, vegetables and eggs. They sell meat from Tablehurst Farm and source from other local biodynamic and organic producers whenever possible. Their range includes juices, sheep and goats' dairy produce, honey and freshly baked bread, cakes and biscuits.

And then there is a place that is a bit tricky to find, but worth discovering. It is commonly known as 'Dave in the Woods' but its name is 'Harvest Supplies'. You'll find it on Marsh Green Lane. Look sharp and you'll see a piece of tree trunk with Harvest Home engraved into it. Go up the track. Turn left at the top and Harvest Supplies is in front of you. I popped in there recently and bought organic Red Pepper & Cashew Spread, Plawhatch yoghurts, celeriac and Romanesco broccoli. They sell everything you could possibly need - wine, cleaning products, shampoo, fruit, vegetables, fresh bean sprouts, pasta, biscuits, bread, milk, cheese, ice cream. And if needed incense and crystals too.

One of the joys of shopping at these farm stalls are the recipes that run through my head when stimulated by the fresh and dry produce on offer, which I know from experience is of outstanding quality. This means that you do not have to do too much to it to let the tastes and flavours sing.

One dish that I like to cook kicks off with the mushroom varieties and the pale gold chickens on offer from Tablehurst, older and slower growing than anything available at a supermarket and raised outdoors. I know it will have the taste of childhood chicken, with massive bones so good for making stock with afterwards. Then there are the huge red onions, the banana shallots and the heads of garlic. Cream, too, is thick and yellow. Celery and young carrots lie piled high and I take some of these too.

Back home, I brown everything in a heavy red Le Creuset casserole pot we've had for decades. Using a mix of butter and olive oil, I first do the onions and the garlic till caramelised with bacon lardons, then the pieces of chicken, browned and crisply caramelised, salted and peppered with rosemary added. Then the finely diced celery and tiny carrots and finally the sliced mushrooms. I cover it all with a good dry cider and a dash of dark soy sauce. I add the cream and place the casserole into in the oven at 160 degrees for an hour and a half. The smells that fill the cottage add to the anticipation of the coming meal. Served with mashed potatoes and a green steamed vegetable, the sauce dolloped over the chicken flecked with bacon and mushrooms, it's a feast for the eye even before you lift a fork. A glass or three of good red wine and a French baguette to mop up the sauce make for a meal that really needs no dessert. But maybe if there is still bread over, why not add to the calorie feast by baking a camembert you cut criss-cross across the top and stud with pecan nuts and prunes? After that, you will need a stiff walk on the Forest or a long afternoon nap.

A wonderful local addition to food shopping comes in the form of food markets and from time to time these include French producers over for the day to sell a fantastic range of the best that their country offers, something that may end now that Brexit has arrived.

The farm we live on has over the years grown a range of varied produce. The fields in front of the cottage used to be a vast cider apple orchard, but this was grubbed up in the 1970s when the farm's new owners went into dairy milk production. When this ended, the land was given over to grass production, wheat, and a small herd of sheep and some Sussex beef cattle. Today the farm produces prime boar, beef, lamb and the odd haunch of venison and offers grass paddocks to the riding and jumping horses, including Callum, that are stabled on the farm.

For an African-born carnivore, there are a number of specialist biltong and dried sausage makers in the area. The biggest and best is Sussmans, just down the road in Newhaven's industrial park. We make visits there now and then to indulge in South African soul food, *boerewors* (farm sausage), dried beef biltong, buttermilk rusks, wines from the Cape, and green fig preserve, tinned guavas, dried fruit rolls and the chocolate bars we grew up with. It's a brilliant way to ignite the tastebuds for a walk down memory lane.

For those of a mind to go foraging for local wild fruit and veg, there are, within a few hundred yards of the cottage, patches of wild garlic, mushrooms, blackberries from the hedgerows and chestnuts galore in season.

The Warren, where we live in Crowborough, got its name as a living larder — a place to raise rabbits in the wild in a constructed warren, a bank of earth with rabbit runs provided, which was regularly harvested using nets and ferrets. But that has long gone now.

We are also well served with vineyards in the area, surprising to a Capetonian, as I would not have thought it warm enough to grow vines. But this tradition, started by the monasteries before they were closed by Henry VIII, has been relaunched very successfully after many centuries. And of course, here in Sussex we lie on the same latitude as Champagne in France. Locally made champagne-method sparkling wine, to the horror of the French, is winning awards and an international following, helped by the fact that it is served on occasion in Buckingham Palace by Her Majesty. One can only wonder what French Presidents and other worthies from across the Channel make of this flag-flying in an industry the French consider their own hallowed turf?

The area is also known for its local cider and huge variety of beers. You need never go thirsty here.

As I've got older, the pleasures of the table have not decreased, if anything just the opposite, but my enjoyment of fine restaurants has faded, due to the cost and to my feeling now and then that I might have done better myself in the kitchen. I love cooking, finding it calming and therapeutic.

But I do enjoy a good pub. I like the egalitarian vibes, the lower prices and the often impressive cooking. When it is safe once more to go back to the pubs, we will doubtless head for The Hatch, The Gallipot outside Hartfield, The Anchor in Hartfield for lunch or supper, or the Coach and Horses at

Chelwood Gate for the superb food and the garden with its views of grazing sheep.

The Griffin Inn at Fletching is a slightly fancy place where Prince Charles has been known to land his helicopter for a pint of Harvey's best bitter and a good meal. The pub's west-facing garden offers great evening sunsets and fish bar-becues at the weekend.

The Neville Crest and Gun on the road to Tunbridge Wells has another good garden and good food and is big enough that you know you will always find a table free. A pub with a French bistro feel, The Hurstwood, is found down a charming country lane in High Hurstwood village. Here there is monkfish, pigs' cheeks, venison, pheasant and pork belly to choose from among many other mouth-watering dishes.

During lockdown, I started baking my own coarse wholemeal bread again as a nice change from the sourdough bread and baguettes which Jan orders in for me alongside jars of my favourite drug, marmalade.

As we enter the third lockdown in this plague year of 2020-2021, the weather on Ashdown Forest is as bleak as it can be after Christmas. There is fog and drizzle, ice and miz-zle. Misery abounds. And for once, I don't have the spirit-lifting exercise involved in looking after Callum. We are housebound, shielding from the virulent new variety of Covid-19. Inevitably, my thoughts turn to marmalade to help me through the winter.

In the lemon light of an English morning, the orange marmalade glows like a church window with the compressed heat of a Spanish summer. In that jar of jellied fruit live a thousand memories of breakfast-in-bed mornings, of sunlight on a woven cream counterpane, of silence, and the rustle of pages turning, of your sun-kissed skin, your copper hair. It is a fragment of time, bittersweet, like the shards of orange peel encased in amber.

Marmalade is an English passion – just how they like it, bottled and kept beneath a lid for safety – a quiet secret indulgence, enjoyed early, with the rest of the day to recover in. It is a passion I share; in this at least we are alike, my no longer new compatriots and I.

There is great pleasure to be had in buying the stuff. It is as various as wine and as the people who make it. There are three-fruit marmalades with lemon, orange and grapefruit, single citrus varieties, and of course there is the crucial factor of cut – the thickness of the peel, coarse, medium or fine. There are light and dark, bitter and sweet, and then there are those marmalade masters, the Scots, who add their own passion to the brew to make a heady whisky-mixed concoction for those special occasions. This is a true mix of the heat of the south and that of the north – a melding of hot and cold passions. No wonder I like it.

This strange stuff has evolved and metamorphosised as it moved north. It was named marmalade by the Portuguese, who ate a version cooked to the consistency of Turkish delight, thick slabs, golden bricks of it, cut thin and eaten with sharp sheep cheese. But it took the English and Scots to make a sweet jam, as we know it, of this bitter fruit. For the orange of Seville and Valencia can be sweet or bitter depending on the variety.

Too much can numb the tongue, too little, and the craving is not assuaged. Ideally it is served on toast, and must not be drowned in butter, but gilded like lip-gloss on a lovely mouth.

Marmalade has greeted me like an old friend in far-flung places where English is spoken and where it is not. I recall it in the vast echoing dining room of an hotel in the northern Cape town of Vredendal, where bare-footed waiters padded silently in to bring breakfasts of bacon and eggs to travelling salesmen, comforted in their distance from home by that silver dish of glinting marmalade. Small packs of it have made airline meals and café breakfasts more bearable. I have eaten it above a red tartan carpet in a small inn on the Scottish coast near Oban. I have had it in Israel and Idaho.

Marmalade is an old, old friend, and one summer I went to its birthplace, the coast near Valencia. Here the orange trees were planted by those other Africans, the Moors, who would little understand the late arrival of a white African from a place five thousand miles south of them.

They came and conquered and stayed and flourished. I came on holiday, a late, a very late, arrival on this much-abused coast, but I too came in search of land, of a place in the sun. But the many cranes, those upside-down 'L's' like punctuation marks emphasizing my lateness, swung about their work of building homes for northerners in search of sun. And the orange groves, glinting a hard dark metallic green in the glare gave ground to white villas and concrete blocks, which will also one day distil a bitter sweetness, I suspect, when the new arrivals tire of sun and heat and foreign ways. And then, perhaps, the orange trees will once more return and their fruit be shipped north again to people who will eat marmalade and remember their southern escapade as they spoon the sticky, shredded jam onto crisp white toast.

We are a secret society, us marmalade eaters, yet the proof of our presence weighs down supermarket shelves everywhere, bulges from displays in specialty food shops and delis. But few know of this passion for the bittersweet; we are protected by the higher profile of the chocoholics and the alcoholics and the biscuit eaters and the doughnut dunkers. Ours is a vice enjoyed in silence at the start of the day, not in smoky nightclubs or in cinema crowds. Our vice comes to us when our palates are refreshed and our systems are awake and tingling with that other friend, the steaming coffee cup.

For some, there is the passion of night, for others there is afternoon delight and then there's us, and our morning madness, for marmalade. It will help me to get through this locked-down winter on Ashdown.

If I have a food fetish, which I freely admit to, it is the result of growing up in two great food-loving traditions. Jewish and Afrikaans cuisine graced the table of my childhood home. The eclectic offerings would include chopped liver, chopped herring, smoked salmon, red herrings, bagels and *kichel*, home-baked corned beef, beef with prunes and carrots, and of course that meal in one, medicine and food combined – chicken soup.

From my mother's Afrikaans heritage would come *bobotie* – curried mince with raisins – barbecued lamb and sausage, every kind of fish, yellowtail, kabeljou, kingklip, red roman, fried, grilled or barbecued, or cold curried fish. There were golden brown chicken pies, venison studded with pork fat and glazed with apricot jam. Smoked duck and smoked sheep ribs. And, being the Cape, there were dried bokkoms – wind-dried mullet – which my father loved, and wind-dried snoek, which I loved, or the pâté made from smoked snoek.

At our holiday home, Just Ashore, at Bloubergstrand, a house washed by the waves at high tide, we were able to land crayfish from the rock pools and kelp right in front of us, cooked in seawater in great tin bathtubs, and served warm with butter and garlic, or cold with mayonnaise.

From the Natal sub-tropics to the north of us came mangoes, paw-paw and lychees. The Cape orchards provided apples, pears, three kinds of peaches, apricots, nectarines, oranges and tangerines.

And the baked desserts were to die for. Milk tart, Cape gooseberry tart, Malva pudding, buttermilk pudding. There were exotic fruit salads studded with passion fruit, and all the melon varieties provided by the Cape in abundance. My father liked to salt his spanspek, the orange-fleshed melon, and my mother liked candied ginger syrup with her green winter melon.

Some of this culinary heritage survives here at home in Sussex. And if I am not careful Callum goes 'Oomph!' as I mount, and I know it's time to ride more and eat less.

COWBOY

I suppose it was inevitable that I would come to think of myself as a cowboy. In my youth, my miles of horse riding, my battered jeans, leather belt with a rodeo buckle, rawhide cowboy boots and a black Stetson helped the image. As I left the stable yard once more just after dawn for a day in the saddle, I would feel my eyes, even behind sunglasses, start to squint against the bright southern African light, the horse beneath me dancing with eagerness to be off to the sea through quiet miles of sand dune and Port Jackson scrub country.

What was missing from this picture were cows. I had no contact with cows and knew nothing about them until I got to England in my 30th year. Then, up on the South Downs in Sussex I ran into them for the first time and they were not at all what I had expected. The image of docile cattle being driven along by cowboys was not what I found. These cattle had minds and personalities and a sense of humour. And a far greater interest in me than I had in them.

The first time Jan and I slipped a gate catch up on the Downs while out riding and found ourselves in a field with a bull was interesting. The bull, it must be said, kept himself to himself and we sidled past, keeping a good hundred yards between us, checking the distance to the next gate and mentally working out whether our horses could jump it if needs be. Luckily, this equation was never put to the test. The bull stayed put, grazing, as we exited his turf.

When out riding, you enter a different space in your head, an older, more primeval consciousness takes over, a sort of fight or flight mechanism which allows you to assess threats more accurately and avoid them, or indeed see them off if need be. When big animals like cattle enter the picture, the horse certainly is on full alert and the rider had best be too.

We found up on the Downs that the trickiest bovine customers were the weaned calves and young stock, who I think simply wished to play with visitors. But being surrounded and chased by young bullocks can be disconcerting, and the horses certainly looked askance at this playfulness.

Having half a dozen red Sussex bullocks crowding your horse at a gate could end badly, so we shooed and waved them away, but this did not seem to deter them overmuch and we had to be prompt in opening those gates and slipping out. Whenever we entered a field up there on the skyline and saw young cattle, we would immediately try to reach the next gate on our ride in a manner which would not start a stampede towards us. It wasn't the easiest thing to judge. If the horses bolted for the gate, the bullocks would think this was a game to which they were invited.

I began to understand that being a cowboy was rather more complicated than it looked on film. My mind took me back to my army days and I recalled some of my farming friends talking about the fun they had riding 'tollies', the newly weaned calves. It was usually a fairly wild ride, I was told, which mostly ended up with the rider lying in a pile of fresh cattle dung. I had no wish to experience this. Nor did our horses.

When we moved our riding base from the Downs to Ashdown Forest, we were very wary at first of the herds of cows with calves afoot that we found there. I'm not sure if these were calmer beasts or whether their being in family groups did the trick, but in all our years of riding on the Forest we've never had a single incident with the cattle. If there is a problem on the Forest, it is when dogs take to chasing sheep.

But the Forest cattle move slowly if at all, brushing away the clouds of flies which beset them, and often sleep under the low tree cover. A horse new to the Forest will take some encouragement at first – Callum was definitely a bit of a nervous Nellie – but in time they learn to live and let live.

Farming advice is that when cows have young calves afoot in spring and early summer, it is the time to be most vigilant. And if you have a dog with you, keep it on a lead, but release it if the cows come for you, as the dog will outrun cows better than you can. At dusk and dawn, it seems cows are more watchful than usual and extra care should be taken at such times of the day.

Over the years I have observed walkers with dogs passing through these cattle on the Forest and have never heard of anything untoward happening.

This is not always the case elsewhere. Stories of dog walkers killed by cows regularly make the newspapers. The dog, it seems, is usually the trigger for the cow's aggression. But not always. A late neighbour of ours, Ron, went to the assistance of a runaway cow on the A26 near the Crow and Gate Pub. He was concerned that the animal would be knocked over by car or a truck. When he finally managed to approach the cow, it charged him, and then knelt on his chest in an attempt to crush him. He was very badly hurt, with broken ribs, and might have died had the cow not got off him. He was lucky to live.

A couple of years ago, a local biology lecturer was trampled to death while walking his elderly Golden Retriever on a farm in Forest Row, when he tried to save his dog. His wife said being trampled by cows had been one of his greatest fears. This is not an unusual occurrence; there are one or two fatalities in the UK each year.

So, when from time to time there are cattle loose on our lane, running together in a tight phalanx like men in a rugby scrum, we step out of the way behind our picket fence pretty smartly. We call our neighbour, Terry, whose charges they are, and he and his Australian cattle dogs and his collie round them up in no time and have them back in their field with the fence mended. It's best to be safe around cattle.

Some years ago, I was walking our black Labrador, Inca, across one of the fields in front of the cottage. I noticed that there were cattle some two fields away and kept walking up the hill to the lane. It was only when we were halfway up the field that I realised the cattle had spotted us, had broken out of their field and were coming for us at the gallop. Inca and I ran for our lives. She reached the gate first of course and dived under it and I hurdled it in a style I would not have believed myself capable of in my sixties. My feet had barely hit the gravel on the far side of the gate when the cattle hit the gate from the other side. Luckily it was robustly built and it held firm. Looking at the restive cattle blowing as hard as I was, I knew in my bones that had they caught up with us I would have been hurt, possibly killed.

On Ashdown Forest, the cattle are generally to be found in the grazing enclosure between the cattle grids on the Nutley Road across the Forest. Despite the weight of motor traffic using the road, you can often see cattle grazing the roadside turf, wandering the road with the resident sheep, or lying beside the road, watching the passing parade in a manner that brings a touch of India to Sussex.

Now and then Callum and I come across cattle spread out across our path in the big bowl or the southern part of the Forest. I wave my whip and shout and shoo them, and they give way with good grace. I am much braver on horseback than on foot. In the summer, they like to congregate around the two Ellison ponds with the causeway between them. The horse and I edge carefully through them, keeping our eyes peeled for any untoward movement, and thus far have always emerged unscathed. But my brush with them while walking Inca stays with me and keeps me on my guard.

A cowboy, it seems, is best up on his horse, not on his feet, when there are cattle about.

FOREST FRIENDS AND ENEMIES

Julian Roup

I must admit that much as I love everything about the Forest, the plants, trees, streams, ponds, and the wildlife, it would not be the enfolding experience it is without the human beings I meet.

One of the pleasures of riding out is the human interaction I get the moment I leave the cottage for the DIY stable next door.

Even after a lifetime of riding, I would not claim to be an expert horseman. But at the yard there are many people whose whole lives have been horses, people who work with them professionally or who have competed at a national and even an international level. They keep you on your toes, and they also do one other thing that is health-inducing and good for the soul and which keeps you grounded. They take the piss a little bit. I cannot complain. I have been known to tease a little myself.

My days, when not in total lockdown, intersect with their lives next door and I am hugely enriched by the experience. I cannot leave the yard without a chat or a word of advice – I've forgotten Callum's overreach boots, my tack could do with a clean, do I want to buy a good second-hand numnah, where am I headed, do I want company, how was my ride, Callum looks well, a three-hour ride, blimey! It is all enriching and entertaining and in lockdown it's been a blessing having this daily interaction albeit from two metres away and lately from behind masks.

There are numerous ways to reach the Forest from home along quiet gravel paths only open to walkers and riders. I know that if I head due south I might run into Susie, an artist, and Ed, an IT guru, or their near neighbours, Maurice, now retired, and Julie, a practice nurse, on their smallholding where they raise their own pigs and beef for the freezer. On the way, I might pass one or two dog walkers or another rider and mostly we just greet each other and continue on our way, but now and again we stop for a chat, the weather, the pandemic, horses, dogs; even politics now and then.

Much as I love riding on my own into the distant reaches of the Forest, if truth be told, I don't really ride alone. With me ride a posse of horsemen and women, some able to ride better than others, but all writers who have inspired me over the years, the travel writers, the nature writers, and the great storytellers who make up the landscape of my mind. These people whisper '*Courage, mon brave, courage*' and stiffen my resolve. Through their eyes I see my own landscape more clearly. And some make me laugh out loud. They are the best of company in the best of times and even more so in the worst. They include Ernest Hemingway and John Steinbeck, Herman Charles Bosman, Barry Lopez, Robert Macfarlane, W.G. Sebald, Richard Mabey, Roger Deacon, Paul Theroux, Jonathan Raban, Siegfried Sassoon, Edith Somerville and Violet Florence Martin, (writing as Martin Ross), Richard Ford, Annie Proulx, Cormac McCarthy and Tim Winton. And so many more, too numerous to mention, whose works have carried me over the humps of life and into near bliss at times. They would be the company I would choose if abandoned on a desert island. And they travel with me as I ride the Forest in all its seasons. They do not know me, yet I count them among the truest of friends.

As a keen fisherman in my youth, I quite often ask the anglers at the lake how they are doing. Invariably they are having a quiet time of it and are no less happy for that, out of the house in the peace and solitude by the water. Recently, though, I met one fisherman, a chef who worked with Marco Pierre White when he took over the Chequers Pub in Maresfield for a time, though it was not a successful experiment. People around here don't seem too keen on fine dining, doing their entertaining at home or in London if that is where they work. We talked fish and fishing of course but also food, and as I rode off, I felt I had met someone, who in time, might become a friend.

I regularly bump into Gary who walks with three Labradors, all beautifully behaved and not needing a leash. We give each other the time of day and talk of weather and mud and dogs and horses.

Now and then I run into our next-door neighbour Terry who is the farm manager responsible for raising the boar, sheep and Sussex cattle on the farm for a restaurant in Tunbridge Wells. Sometimes he is in his truck with his three dogs, the brown Australian cattle dogs and his black and white border collie. We speak of locals and local news and as I ride off, I always feel better briefed on all local doings. Now and then our paths cross when he is leading a group of cross-country motorcyclists. They always pull over as Callum goes dancing past or gives them a twirl just to keep his bloody hand in at this mischief.

Recently, out on the Forest, I met someone who had just read my recent book, *Life in a Time of Plague*, and said she had enjoyed it. This meeting in a thick fog was the first of its kind and I was not a little amazed. Another reader delivered a jar of marmalade to our door, which was home-made and utterly delicious. Both are locals and both ride, so we have much in common.

But there are people that I actively try to avoid, one being the estate manager of the privately owned part of Five Hundred Acre Wood. We've had one or two run-ins and currently the relationship is more cordial than it has been as we discovered that both of us have been in the wars recently, medically speaking. But his presence, patrolling the woods, lends a certain spice and edge to my rides on this patch and I rather like the feeling of playing hide and seek in there.

Now and then I ride out with Zoe, and by the time we have got back to the stables we have pretty much put the world to rights, visited Las Vegas, Cape Town, and covered the problems of raising children and what is on the menu for supper tonight. It is always a bracing conversation and the time simply flies. Now and then she gives me rather despairing advice about collecting Callum who slops along and who frankly I can't be bothered to work on with thighs and calves, it's just too damn exhausting at my age, but I do try for a bit. Zoe pretends not to notice when Callum and I declare a truce and we go back to our old ways of just slopping along in comfort.

Once in a while I bump into non-horsey friends walking their dogs on the Forest and we have a quick catch up on Jan and my doings and theirs. I can see that they are a little nonplussed to meet me on horseback if they have not done so before. Callum usually comes in for much praise and we part ways with spirits lifted all round.

Occasionally I will be stopped and asked for directions by English or even foreign visitors to these parts, and I try my best not to confuse them further. Or I will be stopped by a group of young army reservists out on a map orientation hike. They approach me and the horse with flapping maps that spook the horse and guiltily ask if I can help them to get back to the Crowborough army camp. This request always takes me back to my own cack-handed attempts at map reading in the South African army during my national service and I do my best to assist. One of my downfalls as a map maker or direction giver is that I have given each and every part of the Forest my own name and only Jan will really understand where I mean.

Recently, on returning to the stable after a ride, Zoe was explaining to a fellow rider where we'd been. 'We passed the lake on the far side and turned right at the dogleg, through the gate with the dangerous stakes then up the hill then through the hole in the holly-hedge and down to the pond, through the little zigzag beneath the old pheasant hatchery, then a left at the silver birch with the peeling bark, and then past the fallen pine which tries to impale you as you pass by, up past the house with the ship's gangplank, you know, up the hill from the steam cylinder bridge.' The look of utter mystification on her listener's face told her all she needed to know. The woman did not have a clue and thought Zoe had lost the plot!

Someone I try to avoid when out riding on the Forest is the woman with nine Labradors all running free. If I see her, I take a detour, having had a very unpleasant few minutes with her and her pack when they attacked Callum.

In the midst of the snarling barkfest, I was happy to see that he could take perfectly good care of himself as one or two of the dogs with teeth bared came within kicking distance of his hind feet or chopping distance of his front feet. A menacing leg shake and kick from Callum and they left us alone after that. The woman, however, was caught between wishing to apologise and a strong desire to slap both Callum and me. We exited left, promptly, through the trees.

Over the years I have become reasonably adept at gauging whether dog walkers are friend or foe, and a good 90 per cent are friends one has simply yet to meet. They gather their dogs, stand well back, smile and offer a cheery greeting. The number of good chats I've have with these people add to the pleasure of riding here.

There are two places on the Forest where the ashes of two women lie scattered. I knew one well, the other not at all, but I like to stop by their last resting place and say a quiet hello. Simone Deschamps, the one I knew as a good friend, I fill in on all the horsey gossip I know, nice dogs I've met recently, the latest political news and the state of the steeple chasing world. These were her interests and her touchstones as she battled into her 90th year. By the small wood in which the second woman lies, I just say a quiet prayer and pass on my way.

It is wrong to think of Ashdown Forest as just a collection of trees and heathland. Its human inhabitants add greatly to its interest and I know that if they were not there, I would miss them. Peace, quiet and contemplation are things I treasure, but a landscape without people is a desert of a kind. If this pandemic year has taught us anything, it is that we desperately need people, we need each other to complete our world. This is as true for Ashdown Forest as it is for anywhere on earth.

ASHDOWN AFTER DARK

Julian Roup

Ashdown Forest after dark becomes a very different kind of place. As the dog walkers, family picnickers and horse riders pack up and go home, the Forest seems to breathe a sigh of relief and waits for the night shift to begin.

Over the years, I have had one or two horses that did not object to rides in the dark, particularly on bright moonlight nights, and we have covered miles of the Forest with nobody around, a very different experience to daytime riding.

There is a definite excitement to leaving the stable yard in the dusk before moonrise and heading down the valley to the river bottom as the blue gloaming falls. All birdsong has ended, but there are things in the air, bats that whizz past and owls starting their evening patrols. It is dark beneath the tree cover and every instinct is on high alert, mine and the horse's too. I can feel it in the way he moves; there is none of the slopping along one gets in the light. Now the horse is alert, collected, ready to run if need be. I keep him on a short rein as we jig-jog down the hill.

The river is a dim ripple of sound as we cross the two bridges. I look left into the woods to see if there are any young territorial soldiers coming this way for night manoeuvres but see none and head up the far side of the valley. I wonder if there are any anglers out night fishing on the lake to my right, but the fringe of woodland between the lake and me prevents me seeing. It would be a good night for fishing I imagine; soft and warm.

In a hundred yards, we clip-clop past the lit windows of Ed and Susie's home and later the smallholding of Maurice and Julie. Their two bullocks are stabled for the night.

The vast fields of King's Standing Farm are empty and still, but for one or two pale horse shapes on the far slope. The horse notes them too.

There is a dim finger of light still on the western horizon as we reach the road and cross over quickly to the top of the Forest. As always, when riding at night, my thoughts return to my dapple-grey Irish Draught horse, Chancer, a great night horse, whom I would hold in the middle of the road just long enough for a car's headlights to silhouette us, a naughty instinct that I hoped would provide a thrill to the driver and passengers and maybe start a rumour of a ghost rider on Ashdown. God knows what Chancer and I would have done had we ever met such a rider ourselves?

Out on the Forest proper we are free of tree cover and I look back east to see the full majesty of the rising moon above Crowborough. Just now there is no place on God's earth that I would rather be. We walk on slowly and carefully. Night riding is not about speed but a slow meandering, breathing in the scents and enjoying the peace and quiet.

As the moon rises higher in the sky, I see that we are not quite alone. A solitary walker is headed our way and I rein the horse over to the far side of the path to give him extra passing room. The horse's ears have a lock on him. I greet him, but there is no reply, he just keeps walking. Maybe he is in greater need of silence and privacy than the horse and I this evening. We ride on, heading south and cross the B2026 and descend into the 'Big Bowl'. I am dimly aware of bats but nothing else as the moonlight gilds the gorse and the heather this summer night. At the bottom of the valley we cross the little bridge by the Garden of Eden and for once there are no dog walkers, picnickers or kids playing in the stream. Standing there silently, I can hear the plashing of the little waterfall.

The liquid sound reminds me of the hipflask I have in my inside jacket pocket and reining the horse in, I take a nip of whisky and feel its warmth coursing through me. Now there is definitely a spirit abroad on the Forest, a Scottish one.

It is bright enough now to venture a slow collected trot on the level grassy section between the two splashes and we move along, covering ground. At the dip down into the splash below Friend's Clump I bring the horse back to a walk and we sink into the dappled dark beneath the tree cover, emerging into bright moonlight again on the far side. We turn left and canter softly-softly up the grass ride towards the car park by Ellison's ponds. I pull the horse up at the top of the rise and note there are still a couple of cars in the parking area. The old rumour, that this is Ashdown's Dogging HQ, crosses my mind and I am tempted to ride right up to the cars to give anyone involved an extra thrill, but think twice about that and keep going. It is none of my business. And I think back to my own courting days when a car was the only private place you had to meet a girl in. Peace, joy and pleasure to all involved.

Now we are once more under tree cover in the wooded tunnel that brings you to the two ponds and I keep my eyes open for the cows that like this place. I realize that the horse is doing the very same thing, but this evening there are no cattle, and we cross the causeway silently.

I listen to the few cars passing on the road to my right as we climb up to Camp Hill Clump. As we approach this circle of pines, I hear voices and realise that a young couple is sitting on the bench by the clump. I greet them and they say a very surprised-sounding hello. The horse slows, thinking we are stopping to speak, but I keep him going. Nights on the Forest are private time, not for chatting. Instead, I wave to them and go on my way downhill, being careful of the ruts.

As I ride in silence, I realise how silent my inner world is too. My focus is so much in the present that all my internal chatter has stopped dead and I am just a man on a horse in a vast landscape, focused on the path and the way ahead and on the horse and his mood. The inner dialogue has died away and that in itself is a great pleasure. No noises off.

As I reach our exit gate from the Big Bowl, at its northern extremity, I decide on making the ride into a figure of eight and set off on a second loop even though the horse edges towards the paths that he knows would take him home. He is easily persuaded from them and I aim for the Enchanted Place, entering through the small car park just below it, next to the little quarry. At the top of this hidden car park there is a solitary car, but I can see through its windows in the moonlight that it is empty.

The horse knows where we are headed and that he will get a breather there. We ride into the circle of the Enchanted Place and I dismount on the central stone which bears the bronze plaque commemorating the Pooh Bear author, A.A. Milne and the book's illustrator, E.H. Shepard. I stretch my legs, throw the stirrups up across the saddle to avoid them spooking the horse if he gets a fright. I take one end of the reins, sit on the stone and let my eyes adjust to the view before me, north and west.

A small movement on the grassy ride that circles this hill catches my eye, and I look up at the horse that I can see is also watching it. I focus hard and realise it's a couple on a blanket making love. Probably it is their vehicle in the car park. As silently as possible, I remount and we ghost our way out of there down the hill and then cross the road and head into Five Hundred Acre Wood about a mile further on across the stream and into deep Forest. Now it is much darker, and we move slowly, the Forest scents surround us and the soft sound of the slow sashay of the treetops in the lightest of breezes keeps us company.

For once I am not concerned that I might be caught trespassing here, as it is now past 10pm and if the estate manager is abroad in his Land Rover, I will see his lights well before he spots us, plenty of time for avoiding action, heading deeper into the wood. We stop at the pond and from the height at its eastern end I look down to the moonlit reflections on it. The moon is swimming down there among the tree shadows that cross its surface, lattice-like.

Now and then the horse stops of his own accord, sometimes I can hear movement in the woods, sometimes not, but I can tell by his body language that he has heard something out there, deer, badger, fox or maybe the Sussex Panther. There is no knowing. With a gentle nudge or two from me he starts off again, his easy loping stride eating the miles.

I can hear an owl hunting the grassed rides through the wood. It is an eerie sound and I can't help a slight prickling of my scalp. The horse senses my unease and tenses slightly. As usual, I pat him and sing a line from a lullaby and he relaxes once more.

We ride ever deeper into the wood down towards what used to be the Half Moon pub, now someone's home. As we make the final loop through the wood, heading for home at last, the horse picks up his gait, knowing his stable awaits. He and I are both thinking of home, so at first I don't notice the smell of wood smoke, but then there is no avoiding it. Somewhere close by someone has a fire going. My first thought is that one of the hunters who cull the deer hereabouts has a friendly fire going to keep him company, but soon realise that this is the very last thing he would do. Urging the horse on quietly, we approach the source of the fire. I can now see it and hear it crackling. It is some way back from the path, but its light illuminates a small tent. I am amazed. There is someone camping out here, or maybe this is the more permanent bivouac of a person living wild, the kind of thing one hears of in Wales, where small communities have lasted for years in this way, deep in the woods. This is a path that I seldom take so it may well be that this secret camp has been here for a while.

I am unsure whether it is best to ride on or to retrace my steps to avoid going any closer and spooking the person tending the fire. But that would mean a detour and both horse and I want to get home. We move forward cautiously and thanks to the grassy path, silently, until we've passed the area of the camp. I keep a lookout for anyone about who might be collecting firewood, but there is no one and all is silent but for the owl who continues her patrol.

At Church Hill car park, we cross the road onto our home turf. The car park stands empty and I look up at the twinkling lights of Crowborough on the ridge above us. We hit the path on the valley floor next to the river and follow it to the little stone bridge and the path up the hill to the stables. The horse is keen to have a canter up the hill and as the moonlight shows the way we do just that and soon enough I am dismounting once more. We've been gone for about three hours.

I settle the horse for the night with a brush down and

check his hay and water. I give him a last pat and make my way home to bed. Ashdown after dark has not disappointed, nor has my horse. There is more going on along its miles of trails than one might imagine on this bright moonlight night. I find myself smiling as I head for the cottage.

MIDWINTER SUNSHINE ON ASHDOWN

A sunny day does not mean much to anyone born in South Africa, where sunshine is an almost daily given. Not so in an English winter. Here mid-winter sunshine is a benediction, a passionate kiss, an embrace, a promise of hope, a hint that spring will come, a lifting of spirits, an injection of courage, and a motivation for keeping on keeping on.

You have to live here for some time to appreciate what sunshine means to a human being beset by another biting cold interminable winter. None of us who live in this northbound island are unaware that we live less, live less profoundly, less richly, less in every way in winter. Even those born to this climate suffer.

So when the sun shines on one perfect day in winter as it has been here today, 22 January 2021, we bathe in it, we wash ourselves in its warmth, we eat it, we lift our faces to it and close our eyes as if to a lover. We are the better for it in so many ways. Our batteries are recharged. And we are nicer to each other as a result. The light feels precious as gold.

I walked out into it this morning amid our third lockdown and it was as if I was walking into another country. I had escaped wintertime for a day. It is a feeling that pilots flying internationally experience daily. Breakfast in Mid Sussex and lunch in Marrakesh. As their aircraft punch through the cloud cover, five minutes after take-off from Gatwick, they sit once more beneath the sun.

No such luck for those of us earthbound by work and family. We must endure the long dark days, moving round our homes like moles with here a light, or there, to give us some respite from the gloom. Some days feel like life underwater, the pressure on your chest and heart much the same.

And then one morning you pull back the curtains and like a jewel found in the grass, the sun is rising just beyond the beech trees. And your spirit lifts; your whole body seems to bend towards it and smiles within. I go down the steep cottage staircase that takes you in three tangents first north, then west and then south to the entrance hall and the front door, which I open and step out into the storm porch, opening its door in turn and breathe deeply in the morning air. The sun is creeping round the east of the house which is south facing and will travel its low parabola west keeping the centuries old stone cottage in its shine all day.

A good spot for coffee is the bed, or if you have to be up and doing, then coffee and toast on the couch in the south-facing living room, the small square panes of double-glazed glass seeming to amplify the warmth of the sun, and you sip the steaming coffee and munch the warm toast. The day seems to be filled with promise and you stay put for as long as you can. Basking like a seal freshly beached from the icy grip of the Atlantic.

The day demands a second walk into the sunshine up the lane and a long lean into the sun across a field gate, the sun dazzle behind the eyelids and the gleam on the winter worn fields fringed with the bare beseeching branches of the oaks that seem to beg for sunshine and then the stroll home with the sun-warmth on your back.

Beyond the cottage walls, the Ashdown Forest car parks are suddenly full with walkers and sun seekers. The sun has brought them out in droves, working on their vitamin D-starved metabolisms, like the moon on water, creating high tides, like those before our house on the water's edge in the Cape, so many years ago, bringing fish in schools to fill the tidal pools with teeming life. Now the forest is awash with colour and the shouts of children and the barking of dogs beckoned forth by the sun.

But the cottage is peaceful and lunch is a quiet celebration on the couch in the living room under the window, eating bread and cheese and fruit, the food tasting better for the sunshine condiment spilled out into the ochre-walled room. And then, lying prone on the white couch opposite, a spot drenched by the full sun of afternoon, a dreamless doze and waking to see a sunset that tears at your heart with its beauty beyond the yew tree and the far hills of Ashdown.

As the light dims once more you are filled with a sense of loss, of mourning. A great friend has been visiting and the visit was all that was hoped for and more, but now she is gone.

You go in search of a warm drink to ease the sense of loss and also simply to move out of the brown study you find yourself slipping into. As you walk through the cottage to the kitchen you turn on lights, repelling the falling darkness that seems unquiet and vaguely threatening. The new lit carpets reflect bold colours back to you in reds and yellows, royal blue and gold, and after making the hot mug of tea you walk back to the lamplit living room, warming your hands around it and the mug.

The sunset has faded but a soft glow still provides a tree silhouette, a tracery of branches beyond the windows. You sip the warmth and close your eyes and try to recall the sun dazzle of your departed friend. It has been a holiday of sorts amid the bleak weeks of midwinter.

The thought comes to me that though we don't see the sun that often here in winter, our joy at its appearance is maybe worth the cost of living in the dark. We never get the chance to take it for granted as we do with so much in this life from too much ice cream which palls after a while or too many visitors.

When the sun is with us, the sacred link with the sky is acknowledged afresh, our dependence on it and our love for it as for a mother, which in a way it is. Recharged and re-energized by its appearance we plod on through the winter gloom, our covenant with the sky renewed, faith in our hearts once more that our friend the sun will be back with us before long to celebrate spring. And all shall be well, and all shall be well, and all manner of things shall be well.

ASHDOWN'S PLAGUE YEAR

This year Britain and indeed the whole world has ridden into the dark Secret Heart of the Forest, metaphorically speaking.

And there we have found many terrible things – incompetence, short-sightedness, corruption, greed, selfishness and cruelty. But we have also found out there on the twisted paths through the woods, the kindness of strangers, the dedication and bravery of the staff of the NHS, the help and support of neighbours, shelf-stackers and pharmacists, all the people manning essential shops, teachers, dustbin men, postmen, petrol station staff and heroic delivery drivers, to mention just a few. They have kept us going. And, of course, the scientists who have found us vaccines that will allow life to return to this blighted land are also among our heroes.

This plague year has taught us many salutary lessons, not least of which is that our Government has failed us in the most profound way. With 100,000 dead from Covid-19 at the time of writing this (14 January 2021), Britain has truly become the sick man of Europe.

But Covid-19 has also brought gifts, reminding us profoundly of the importance and pleasure that other people mean in our lives as we've sat cooped up in our homes unable to meet with grandparents, parents, siblings, children, grandchildren and friends. And we have learned afresh the healing power of nature, of the help it offers to the stressed, the tired and the mentally ill. How did we ever forget? I've thanked my lucky stars, daily, that I have the privilege to live on Ashdown Forest, which has been an island of sanity in a nation mad with suffering and loneliness.

The rammed Forest car parks, the family groups picnicking, the increased numbers of walkers and riders, are all indications of the importance of Ashdown to so many people. They have come here seeking space to breathe, free to commune with nature, to look beyond the confines of four walls, to touch plants and yes, to hug trees. And maybe to pray for the strength to endure the new added pressures of this plague year, its lockdowns and the fear of death stalking the land. I have no doubt that each visitor went home just a little comforted and easier in their minds.

After the First World War in 1918, Prime Minister Lloyd George made a legendary speech in Wolverhampton in which he called for making Britain 'a fit country for heroes' as a way of thanking the troops for their sacrifice. He promised better housing and other benefits. Sadly, few of these promises materialised.

After the Second World War, British voters decided that they wanted a different kind of country. Out of that feeling the NHS was born. Maybe this feeling will be repeated after this catastrophe, which has left Britain the hardest-hit nation in Europe. We cannot see it yet, but there may be a silver lining to all this death and suffering. Voters may demand a better Britain.

We need leaders who will ensure that next time we are better prepared for disaster. As we move through the 'Pandemic Forest', a new dawn is breaking. We need to see again how beautiful this world is and that there are indeed magic money trees in the Forest, trees that can, if we have the wish and the will, provide for every last man, woman and child in this country. No more homeless, no more hungry, no more people living in abject poverty, no more slaves working in plain sight. We need to narrow the gap between the haves and the have-nots. If we manage to do these things, then the 100,000 dead may rest a little more peacefully. These things will stand as their best memorial.

Each day during this hellish year, as I have turned from the political and medical news to the rides I've had on the Forest in this time of lockdown and the 40 years before, I think that they have been a kind of arboreal therapy. Forest soul-bathing. The mix of fresh air, exercise, beauty, wilderness, quiet and contemplation, the scenery and the wildlife have been a form of moving meditation. Through the collapse of relationships, the death of parents and loved ones, health disasters, job losses, the stresses of raising a family without any family support network, money troubles. The stuff that life throws at all of us, the stuff our failed education system should prepare us for but does not even touch on, these things were all made bearable by riding on the Forest. Each ride came with a gift of happiness and the offer made that you could choose to be happy even as despair threatened to engulf you. The Forest has been a lifesaver. It has also been an inspiration to me as a writer. From its woods have come stories that have seemingly reached me like leaves in autumn falling from the trees as I rode through them. It has given me this book and others too.

If you walk across Pooh Sticks Bridge and look low down on the trunks of the oak trees you will see the windows and doors of the mythical animals of this storied place. Children leave small jars of honey for Pooh Bear and his friends by each door. I am not sure who collects them and what becomes of them. But like the Tooth Fairy and Father Christmas, this is a story which has gripped the minds of generations of children. It is magic of the best kind, a bringing together of a child's mind and the wild woods. What could be better? This link starts a love for nature and animals that could be the salvation of our world in the same way that acorns lead to oaks.

I know deep within me that my time is running short, much as I wish to deny it. At any moment I expect to hear the call of 'Time's up!' I have written elsewhere in *A Fisherman in the Saddle*:

> 'But one day it must end, I know that. There will come a day when riding on Ashdown, deep in its hidden heart, is part of my past rather than the centre of my present. It will be a sad day. A great pleasure will have gone, and maybe me with it.
>
> 'One cannot ride for as long as I have ridden – near 65 years – in the Cape, in California, and on Ashdown Forest in Sussex, and not think, once in a while – how will it end? When it comes it may be swift, or it may be

just that aching bones and arthritis keeps me by the fireside. The trick is to continue for as long as possible, in the same way that a horse kept in work, keeps working. That is my plan. Life may plan differently.

'What is certain is that it will end one day, as I know in my heart it must. It may be that 'It' will wait for me by one of the little wooden bridges that cross the Forest streams, funnelling riders and walkers across its many web-like paths. I will take 'It' for a walker in hiking boots and anorak. But 'It' will not be a walker. There will be a slip, a fall, a pain and with luck it will all be over. Maybe I will be reunited with all my lovely old friends, the horses that have been so much of my story, once more, Duke at their head.

'It may not be that quick. It may be a fall and a foot caught in a stirrup, bumping along the side of a terrified horse, dragged back to the stables unrecognisable. I sincerely hope not.

'It may be that I will have to sell my last horse and see him go away to another place to carry someone else in strange country. That too will be hard.

'As I ride here in my new homeland, my old one is ever before my eyes. That is the bifocal view of exile or emigration. Ashdown has been my Africa. The miles of rusty, winter-dry bracken the Transvaal, Five Hundred Acre Wood, dense with chestnut, beech and oak, is indisputably the Cape; the wild open spaces of brown winter-burned heather and lion-coloured grass, the Karoo and the Free State; away in the mist, the line of the Downs, the Tygerberg Hills; the sea in the far distance is still, still the Atlantic, but north, not south.

'As I ride, my two worlds glide together and mix, kaleidoscope-like. I sing Afrikaans lullabies to an Irish horse, in England. And the strange thing is, he understands. He too is an exile, his roots in Ireland, his birthplace far distant. We, all of us, must learn to adapt to new ways and new places; after all, life's only constant is change.

'My horses have been my friends, my constant companions, my confidantes, my medicine, my means of escape from the pressing needs of the 'real world', so described by those that run it. They would, wouldn't they?

'Horses are a quick way through the looking glass to the world behind, beyond, to the Faraway Tree, to magic. They have hugely enriched my life. They have lent me rhythm and rhyme, poetry and song, good health and a better heart rate. They have driven me half crazy, both with joy and fear. They have taught me my limits - oh what a good lesson that! They have shown me the way to the stars. They have taught me something of humility and kindness, patience and content. They have made me be still, even in motion. The gift of riding is a gift beyond price.

'I will be sorry when riding ends; but if that end is not also my own, what golden seams of memory I will mine. No squirrel seeking his winter hoard will find greater riches. I will remember the horses on quiet nights as the winter land lies stilled, and summer friends long gone. Horses bedded on straw and cats lying quiet on corduroy. Pheasants strutting the lanes away from huntsmen-haunted woods; stored chestnuts and leaves that rustled, fermenting now on Forest floors. The sun will be gone and with it work. The winter land is still. And so, finally, am I.'

The Forest has so many lessons, so many gifts for us, we must treasure it. And the best thing is that it is there for us, tomorrow and tomorrow and tomorrow. Enter it and be charmed and enraptured, open your soul to it and you will be enriched. Ride into the Secret Heart of the Forest and you will be changed by it, forever.

Julian Roup
East Sussex
14 January 2021

Maxwell's Summer
By M. J. Trow

Peter Maxwell is looking forward to a nice quiet summer, with perhaps a little light gardening if necessary – as long as the plants don't grow over the door and trap them all inside, it won't be necessary. But, as so often in Maxwell's life, Mrs Troubridge happens and a day out for her and her special friend, Mrs Getty, takes Maxwell and Nolan to Haledown House and from there into a web of intrigue and death.

Maxwell's Summer turns out to be nothing like he planned. As resident conversationalist at a stately home, with riding lessons on the side for Nolan and free dinners when she wants them for Jacquie, Mad Max Maxwell could be forgiven for expecting a pretty easy time of it – with a nice fat cheque thrown in. But murders soon cross his path – almost literally – and with his own life in danger, will he even make it to the dreaded A Level Results Day?

Closing Time
By Various Authors

They say a stranger is just someone you haven't met yet.

But chance works in mysterious ways.

Several strangers end up at *The Whistler* on Saturday night, a popular pub in London's vibrant and cosmopolitan Soho district.

These strangers will find, when the clock strikes 22:22, that fate and circumstance has linked and intertwined them in ways they could never have imagined.

Welcome to *The Whistler*, we hope you enjoy your stay.

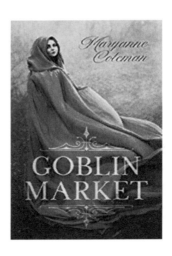

Goblin Market
By Maryanne Coleman

Have you ever wondered what happened to the faeries you used to believe in? They lived at the bottom of the garden and left rings in the grass and sparkling glamour in the air to remind you where they were. But that was then – now you might find them in places you might not think to look. They might be stacking shelves, delivering milk or weighing babies at the clinic. Open your eyes and keep your wits about you and you might see them.

But no one is looking any more and that is hard for a Faerie Queen to bear and Titania has had enough. When Titania stamps her foot, everyone in Faerieland jumps; publicity is what they need. Television, magazines. But that sort of thing is much more the remit of the bad boys of the Unseelie Court, the ones who weave a new kind of magic; the World Wide Web. Here is Puck re-learning how to fly; Leanne the agent who really is a vampire; Oberon's Boys playing cards behind the wainscoting; Black Annis, the bag-lady from Hainault, all gathered in a Restoration comedy that is strictly twenty-first century.

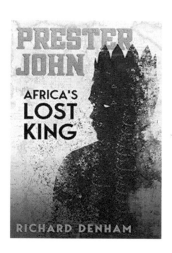

Prester John: Africa's Lost King
By Richard Denham

He sits on his jewelled throne on the Horn of Africa in the maps of the sixteenth century. He can see his whole empire reflected in a mirror outside his palace. He carries three crosses into battle and each cross is guarded by one hundred thousand men. He was with St Thomas in the third century when he set up a Christian church in India. He came like a thunderbolt out of the far East eight centuries later, to rescue the crusaders clinging on to Jerusalem. And he was still there when Portuguese explorers went looking for him in the fifteenth century.

He went by different names. The priest who was also a king was Ong Khan; he was Genghis Khan; he was Lebna Dengel. Above all, he was a Christian king who ruled a vast empire full of magical wonders: men with faces in their chests; men with huge, backward-facing feet; rivers and seas made of sand. His lands lay next to the earthly Paradise which had once been the Garden of Eden. He wrote letters to popes and princes. He promised salvation and hope to generations.

But it was noticeable that as men looked outward, exploring more of the natural world; as science replaced superstition and the age of miracles faded, Prester John was always elsewhere. He was beyond the Mountains of the Moon, at the edge of the earth, near the mouth of Hell.

Was he real? Did he ever exist? This book will take you on a journey of a lifetime, to worlds that might have been, but never were. It will take you, if you are brave enough, into the world of Prester John.

Fade
By Bethan White

There is nothing extraordinary about Chris Rowan. Each day he wakes to the same faces, has the same breakfast, the same commute, the same sort of homes he tries to rent out to unsuspecting tenants.

There is nothing extraordinary about Chris Rowan. That is apart from the black dog that haunts his nightmares and an unexpected encounter with a long forgotten demon from his past. A nudge that will send Chris on his own downward spiral, from which there may be no escape.

There is nothing extraordinary about Chris Rowan...

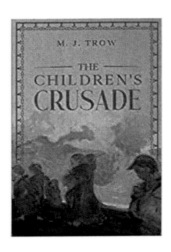

The Children's Crusade
By M. J. Trow

In the summer of 1212, 30,000 children from towns and villages all over France and Germany left their homes and families and began a crusade. Their aim; to retake Jerusalem, the holiest city in the world, for God and for Christ. They carried crosses and they believed, because the Bible told them so, that they could cross the sea like Moses. The walls of Jerusalem would fall, like Jericho's did for Joshua.

It was the age of miracles – anything was possible. Kings ignored the Children; so did popes and bishops. The handful of Church chroniclers who wrote about them were usually disparaging. They were delusional, they were inspired not by God, but the Devil. Their crusade was doomed from the start.

None of them reached Outremer, the Holy Land. They turned back, exhausted. Some fell ill on the way; others died. Others still were probably sold into slavery to the Saracens – the very Muslims who had taken Jerusalem in the first place.

We only know of three of them by name – Stephen, Nicholas and Otto. One of them was a shepherd, another a ploughboy, the third a scholar. The oldest was probably fourteen. Today, in a world where nobody believes in miracles, the Children of 1212 have almost been forgotten.

Almost… but not quite…

The poet Robert Browning caught the mood in his haunting poem, *The Pied Piper of Hamelin*, bringing to later readers the sad image of a lost generation, wandering a road to who knew where.

www.blkdogpublishing.com

Printed in Great Britain
by Amazon